ONE WOMAN'S ADVENTURE

From

Hitler's Germany
to
the Cross of Christ

and Beyond ...

Friede McDonald Taylor
with Jack Taylor

Foreword by R.T. Kendall

Cover art by Amanda Grace Butt

www.BurkhartBooks.com

Bedford, Texas

Endorsements

"Jack and Friede Taylor are two of the most authentic disciples of Jesus I've ever met. They exude the wisdom, passion, and love of Jesus to all who meet them. You are sure to be impacted by this powerful story, *From Hitler's Germany to the Cross of Christ. . . and Beyond.*"

Bill Johnson
Bethel Church, Redding, CA
Author of *When Heaven Invades Earth* and *God is Good*

"I have known something of the thrilling story of the providence of God in bringing Jack and Friede together. This is proving to be a key relationship in the Kingdom of God as she and Jack, my spiritual father for many years, travel the world in ministry together. This book will provide a thrilling reference for everyone seeking to navigate the world by Kingdom principles."

Randy Clark, D. Min. Th.D.
Founder, Overseer of Global Awakening Network

"Not only does *From Hitler's Germany to the Cross of Christ* provide a firsthand glimpse into a tragic part of world history, it gives you a look into the intriguing history of one woman. If you think God is not still at work personally changing lives and families, you need this book. If you wonder whether it's worth trying to start over again after having failed, you need this book. If you've given up hope and consider your past irredeemable, your present life a drudgery, and your future uncertain, then take hope from Friede Taylor's life. Her story of overcoming a past of rejection, abuse, and tragedy may not be exactly like your own, but the most important part of her story—that God cares and will meet you wherever you are—will ring true for anyone."

Jen McDonald,
Author of *You Are Not Alone: Encouragement for the Heart of a Military Spouse*

"If you are interested in reading about a oft-forgotten story, one of courage, one of deliberate survival, and ultimately a testimony of God's grace through His never ending mercies and provision, then this book is for you! Friede is a walking testimony to the beauty of the narrative that is woven from a life given to the Father and is beautifully detailed in the pages of this book. She is my confidant, my friend and my sister!"

Jennifer Hilderbrand Hetland,
Wife, Mother and Children's Book Author

"Why are we drawn to stories of heroic triumph over seemingly impossible circumstances? When Friede joined me on a trip to Mozambique several years ago, and was lovingly pressured, pushed, into sharing; she shared this story, in a nutshell. I watched as the atmosphere shifted and the tears flowed. It has been an honor and joy to walk with her and her sweet husband who together have become my spiritual parents and continue to cheer me and my family on in life and ministry!"

Leif Hetland,
Author, International Speaker

"Friede Taylor's skill in telling her German family's escape during Hitler's murderous rampage across Europe will lock-in your attention in an unforgettable way. Born as an unwanted child to a father devoted to the Nazi war-machine, Friede's life began in a reign of terror and rejection. Fleeing the Allied blitz of Germany her mother escaped with her to Austria, only to find themselves trapped again. The Allies were advancing from the West; the Russians were coming from the East. There was no place to hide, no refuge of peace. The War ended abruptly, Germany lay in total ruins, and Friede grew up in those perilous post-war times. Even after her marriage to an American soldier and move to the United States, the pattern of grief continued to stalk her. Finally, it was in the midst of family crisis that Friede met Jesus Christ. That awesome day, He changed everything. She experienced what Wesley described in a hymn: Her chains fell off, her heart was free, she rose, went forth, and followed Thee.

Friede's transition from grief to grace is in the story before you. Read it with reverence. It is the true life-story of a courageous woman you hold in your hands."

Charles Carrin,
Author, Conference Speaker, and member of the
WordSpiritPower Team with R. T. Kendall & Jack Taylor

"Be ready to weep and be encouraged as you read the incredible account of God's faithfulness over this woman's life. Why do we need these testimonies today? We need them retold as the mothers and fathers of Israel retold their own story, to remember and to call forth the faithfulness of God again and again in our lives and in the lives of those we love. Friede's story longs to be used as a catalyst for God to do again what He has done for her."

Gail B. Hawkins,
Pastor, New Life City, Albuquerque, NM

"Friede's story is captivating! Repeatedly, tears of sadness filled my eyes being stunned by the tragedies of life she artfully discloses. Without this written account one would never know what Friede has endured. I can say first handedly, the author isn't a victim of life but a victor in Christ. I love you Friede, and am deeply grateful for your love for dad, and your acceptance and love for my family."

Tamara Taylor Snell,
Executive Assistant, Grace Church, Orlando, FL

"It is an honor to endorse this living epistle memoirs to anyone who desires to see the Father actively orchestrating His plan in a persons life. Her early life's journey is like something you would read out of the Book of Acts. What a Lady of God, here are some characteristics of her life that speak to me. First, is loyalty to the Kingdom's work. From the early years serving Leif Hetland I have viewed this quality. Second, Her anointing to minister Our Lord's healing touch in the life of so many in which Auburn Heights Baptist Church has been the beneficiary. Finally, the Bible says when a man finds a wife he finds a good thing. My spiritual Papa Dr. Jack Taylor's life has been rejuvenated by the presence of this Lady of God in his life. His health and vitality speaks of a Woman of God in the house. With honor I recommend this book and this Lady to the church. Truly a sign and wonder for proof of God's Grace."

Dr. Wayne Scarborough,
Sr. Pastor, Auburn Heights Baptist Church, Phenix City, AL

Dedication

I dedicate this book to …

The memory of my Mama, Maria Dedeo Vojtech Voss, who always had a song in her heart and taught me to never give up hope.

The memory of my son Gene, whose story will bless every reader.

My husband Jack, who is showing me the meaning of a Kingdom marriage.

My children Sheila, Steve, and wife, Jennifer without whom this book would not be possible.

My grandchildren: Dakota with husband Mark, Matthew with wife Jeramae, Raquel, Gabriel with wife Brittney, Cecil, Grace, and Anna.

My Great-grandchildren Lillian Ruth, Charles Lloyd, and Leila Grace.

Leif and Jennifer Hetland, who loved me into the spiritual life and took me under their wings, showed me how to live accordingly by their example. Without them, I would not be where I am today.

To all the above: I Love You!

Contents

Foreword by R.T. Kendall

I remember as though it was yesterday. I was standing in the second row and Jack Taylor was standing directly in front of me. In the midst of the praise service at Christ Chapel, in Florence, Alabama on a fall October night, Jack suddenly turned and walked into the aisle toward the back, a dozen rows or so.

I learned the next day that he had walked back to where Friede McDonald was standing with her hands lifted in praise. She reported later that when she saw Jack leave the front, she heard the words in her mind, "If he asks you to marry him, you will say, 'Yes!'"

Regularly, during such a conference, Jack, Charles Carrin and I gather in a team meeting for prayer and discussion regarding the coming sessions of the *WordSpiritPower* conferences. It was obvious to both Charles and me that Jack seemed to have something he wished to discuss with us. He had spent several hours the evening before talking with Friede. I was not expecting what followed, namely, an immediate and definite witness that Jack should marry Friede. Seldom in my life have I ever gotten such a clear witness as this from the Holy Spirit. And I had the nerve to tell Jack on the spot. But alas, to my surprise, I was late! Jack had already asked her to marry him!

Now, it wasn't that they were perfect strangers. He had known Friede from years past when she was personal assistant to Leif Hetland. In fact, when Jack's first wife, Barbara died, Leif had thought he had heard from God that Friede and Jack belonged together. Jack remarried a year later to Jerry, who was found with cancer during their engagement period and died after only twenty-one months of marriage. Of course, Jack was even more grieved than before.

Again, the next evening I walked over to Friede during the conference session, intending to treat her like family—since I was convinced that she would be marrying Jack. I forgot to put on a smile before I spoke and, rather frankly, said to her, "You need to know that you need to come through me if you want to get to Jack Taylor!" I was to learn later that I nearly scared her into backing out of the whole thing! I was joking! (That taught me a lesson—to make sure that my countenance was not so serious when I was teasing someone). For years she was afraid of me, even though I was joking.

These things said, Jack and Friede have been married now more than eleven years and she has been a part of mine and Louise's lives all this time.

Jack, Charles, and I have been part of the *WordSpiritPower* team since 2001 and have had over seventy-five meetings from England and Canada and from the Carolinas to Texas and New Mexico.

Friede honored me when she asked me to write this Foreword, I immediately said, "Yes!" but I was not prepared for how good this book is.

You are probably not prepared for what is coming. What you are about to read is one of the most thrilling, gripping, stunning and heart-warming pieces of literature you have read in your lifetime. I guarantee it! You won't be able to put it down. I myself did not know half the things she has said in this book. It is Friede's autobiography. Born in Czechoslovakia and brought up in Germany, she speaks with courage and candor of a girl who was not loved by her father and knew only disdain from him all her life.

Friede is a gifted writer and takes the reader with her through her fascinating life with intrigue and inspiration.

God bless you as you read this book. It will make you want to get closer than ever to God.

R.T. Kendall
Author, Conference Speaker, and former Pastor of
Westminster Chapel in London, England

Foreword by Jack Taylor

The little baby was born in crisis times; her birth was both unplanned and unwanted. Her father, Karl, later a soldier in Hitler's feared and vicious Waffen-Schutzstaffel, the Fuehrer's armed wing of the Nazi party, wanted a boy. So Friede's entry into the world began with disappointment and was met with rejection. Her father must have had great excitement about adding another male child to the family so his four-year-old son, Roland, could have a playmate. There was one daughter already and in Karl's mind, it was time for another boy. His disappointment was keen and would soon ramp into disdain, a feeling that would play a major role in the coming years for both daughter and father. For almost twenty years Friede never felt her father's love, respect or admiration. To the contrary, she heard words and witnessed acts of unkindness, punishment, criticism, and rage. She will report of this conflicted youth in the early chapters of this book. Not to condemn her father but to glorify Jesus, Who one day would be her Savior.

With her mother, Maria, the relationship was totally different. Maria loved her children with equal gentleness and made it obvious in every conceivable way. She was beautiful, aristocratic and a talented classical pianist who lived, against all odds, in undying hope.

Friede contracted both cholera and typhoid fever early in her life because of poor sanitation and lack of nourishment, and as a baby was hospitalized in serious condition. So sick, so long with no improvement, the hospital staff made the decision to discharge the dying baby to the care of her mother, dismissing her as a patient. Her chances to live were slim to none, and the hospital needed her bed. But where would Friede, her mother, Maria, and her brother and sister, live? They had no home, no help, and no hope. The baby needed blood, and without it death was certain. The city of Bratislava lay in ruins from Allied bombs and offered no alternative refuge for the desperate family.

In crisis times angels seem to appear. This time an angel, in the person of a nurse, heard the conversation of the baby's plight, stepped up and into the life of this family. The nurse took the baby to her home, where she fed the baby with her own food, and even give the baby her own blood.

Later, as the family was fleeing to Austria, Karl was suddenly and without warning drafted into Hitler's failing army to serve in the feared Waffen-Schutzstaffel (better known as the Waffen-SS, the armed wing of the Nazi Party's Schutzstaffel—"Protective Squadron"). Though her father would return to the family at the end of the war, his relationship of disfavor continued. He was not there for the baby and would never be. This attitude toward his baby daughter was a ghost that would torment her all her life until she met Jesus.

Thus began the story being told here of trouble, terror, rejection, poverty and yes, ultimately, providence. A provident God was watching the story as it began to unfold and, as always, behind the scenes with methods, events, wars and want, God was working to bring a life to an amazing level of meaning and significance. It is a wonderful story, warm and warming to all who have been and will be touched by it.

Down line, half a century later by the grace of God, I became part of this saga.

I am Jack Taylor and that baby, saved from certain death by Providence, is now my wife, Friede McDonald Taylor.

And now, the rest of the story!

Jack Taylor

One Solitary Woman

A Tribute to My Mama from Jack

Maria Dedeo Vojtech Voss was a woman the whole world should have known. Anyone who might have known her would have been influenced by her goodness. When the final bell rings to sound the end of time, if truth be known, Maria Voss will very likely be listed among the heroines of the centuries.

She was born Maria Dedeo February 26, 1915, the third child of Hermann and Marie. Within a few days of her birth, her mother died. She gave her daughter life but, in the process, lost her own. Subsequently, her father married her mother's sister, and they had eight more children, altogether consisting of eleven children, ten girls, and one boy.

Maria lived in Bratislava for the first 30 years of her trouble-laden life. She was married to Karl Vojtech in 1936, and they raised four children, Friede, being the third child. Maria's husband was an excellent tailor with a thriving business, but his success was marred by seasons of depression that limited his keen abilities. These depressive episodes were likely the result of the war in which his business was totally destroyed. These losses influenced his life, disposition and family relationships. In these seasons Maria was forced to care for the family as well as the business. Her willingness to do this developed in her a lifestyle of confident responsibility and compassionate care. Though Karl was present in the home during those seasons, there was virtually no communication with the family. As will be reported later, Karl, Maria's husband, and Friede's father, took his own life, which in all likelihood, was precipitated by his propensity toward deeper depression, likely due to the destruction of his entire business in the war. Maria's life was never an easy one, before or after her husband's death. It is easy to assume that a proper response to her unfortunate surroundings brought her to a condition of betterment rather than bitterness.

Our Initial Visit

I first visited this remarkable woman on my initial visit with Friede to her native Germany in 2005. She was my mother-in-law. To be in her presence was to sense her settled kindness, her warm unpretentiousness, and her total acceptance. Any attempt to put herself forward or impress others was noticeably absent. I was a stranger and, though separated by the barrier of language, we found ourselves very comfortable with one another. As Friede will report later, I had memorized the Aaronic Blessing from the Bible in the German language and early in our visit spoke the blessing to Maria in her own language. I was sure I did well when, the next morning, she asked Friede if I would do it again. Thus, we rapidly bonded.

An Amazing Revelation

Maria was a Catholic from her childhood and had requested that Friede never leave the Catholic Church. Being Catholic, she was never led to believe in a personal experience of salvation. Friede had been soundly converted to Christ in America and was wonderfully filled with the Spirit and became a powerful witness to Jesus. Thus, she was concerned about her Mother's conscious relationship with God through Christ. Each time, when she visited her mother, she would say something like, "Mama, if we don't see each other here on earth again, I will see you later in heaven." Her response on each occasion was, "I hope so." Later, during a subsequent visit, Friede led her mother to faith in Jesus. Her mother was ninety-one! At the end of that visit, Friede spoke her usual final words, proposing, "Mama, I will see you later, here or in heaven." Her mother's quick and clear response was, "Yes!"

The revelation of which I speak has to do with a person's character before a personal experience with Jesus takes place. In Maria's case, she had been brought up with the truths of God, the death and resurrection of Jesus and heaven and hell. Though she intellectually believed in the facts about God and Jesus, she had never encountered Jesus as Savior. Yet, though unconverted, her character was shaped by the truths she believed, and these simple beliefs accepted and applied, carried this woman to greatness. I saw that greatness before she came to know Jesus Christ as Savior.

When Friede speaks of her mother, it becomes clear that her mother's character and lifestyle were powerful influences in every stage of her life. In a season of the ravages of war, poverty and conflict, her faith in the providences of God never wavered. She had probably never read the book of Proverbs, but she was a "Proverbs 30" woman:

"A wife of noble character who can find? She is worth far more than rubies" (v. 10).

Read the list of qualities of such a woman:

"Her husband has full confidence in her ...." (v. 11).
"She gets up while it is dark, provides food for her children and portions for her servants" (v. 15).
"She sets about her work vigorously; her arms are strong for her tasks" (v. 17).
"She opens her arms to the poor and extends her hands to the needy" (v. 20).
"When it snows, she has no fear for her household for all of them are clothed in scarlet" (v. 21).
"She is clothed in strength and dignity; she can laugh at the days to come" (v. 25).
"She speaks with wisdom and faithful instruction is on her tongue" (v. 26).
"She watches over the affairs of her household and does not eat the bread of idleness" (v. 27).
"Her children rise up and call her blessed" (v. 28).
"Give her the reward she has earned, and let her works bring her praise" (v. 28).

These words form an apt description of Maria Voss, mother of Friede, my wife.

You see, I am pleasingly prejudiced toward her because Friede continuously honors her as the greatest influence on her life, outside Jesus Christ Himself. Maria never lost her song; she never relented to hopelessness, and she never flagged in her zeal to live life to the fullest or in her determination to prepare her household for the rigors of life.

Of all the things I could say about this great woman, I believe that when all is said and done, among her greatest contributions to the world will be the life of her daughter, Wilfriede Voss McDonald Taylor. Long before Maria met Jesus Christ as Savior, she was instinctively and lovingly shaping Friede's life. Though her voice has been silenced in death, she continues to speak through Friede as she articulates so beautifully the Gospel of Jesus Christ in word and deed.

It is to this woman, Maria Dedeo Vojtech Voss, that I pay tribute, and to whom, among others, Friede dedicates this book.

Jack Taylor
(Better known as Friede's husband!)

Introduction

I was born in Bratislava, Czechoslovakia prior to the end of World War II. In January of 1945, our family fled Czechoslovakia for Austria and later to Germany because the Russian army was advancing and there was fear that we would fall into the hands of what was then the dread enemy of Germany. Because I was a baby, there was no recorded memory of those days. I have had to depend on others for needed specifics.

Explanation from My Mama

As I visited my mother years later, she would share some details of this turbulent season:

"We fled Bratislava in an open truck in the dead of winter in hopes of reaching Pressbaum where my grandparents and aunts lived. Because our journey took us through Vienna, we had to try to take shelter due to bomb threats and advanced very slowly. When we finally reached Agsbach, we decided to take shelter at my uncle's house who was the head forest ranger in the area. After we arrived there, your father, suddenly and without warning, was drafted into Hitler's Waffen-SS, apparently part of a last-ditch effort to keep the Nazi cause from crumbling altogether. He was transported to Vienna. I remained in Agsbach with my uncle and aunt and my little family without your father.

When in March 1945 the rumor went around that the Russians were in Baden near Vienna, approximately thirty kilometers from Agsbach, my uncle fled with his family toward Tyrol, Austria while I remained alone in their house with you and your siblings. Later that evening my uncle's forest assistant returned from his vacation and found only me with my children.

Because the Russians kept advancing nearer to where we were staying, the forest assistant took us another two kilometers through the forest into a settlement consisting of soldiers of the "Wehrmacht" (the unified armed forces of Nazi Germany) in hopes to keep us hidden. You, dear Friede, were still in a little baby carriage. Out of fear of being captured by the Russians, the forest assistant immediately left again, leaving us there alone. Within a few days, we left there in hopes of reaching the city of Pressbaum where my grandparents and aunts lived. When we arrived there, they would not take us in because they feared that the Russians, who had raged there before, would return again. Instead, they referred us to the next village of others who had also fled from Bratislava in hopes that they would give us shelter. There we were allowed to stay a few days with a young family who had four children of their own. They suggested that I go to the mayor's office in town to get groceries for us. When I arrived there, I received no food but instead was arrested and handed over to the Russian authorities. They, in turn, took me to a Russian prison camp far away from Vienna for interrogation to find out whether I had been a member of the National Socialist German Workers Party (NSDAP), also known as the Nazi Party and constantly threatened me at gunpoint in case I made an attempt to flee. Because we had lived in Czechoslovakia, we knew nothing about any German Party. Since we had a tailor salon in Bratislava, we were under Slovak supremacy and therefore, never under German policy. During this time, you and your brother and sister were without food. This was in May of 1945.

After two weeks I was brought back to Pressbaum at gunpoint where the officers examined all my belongings without finding whatever they were looking for and ordered me to take my children and leave immediately for Vienna."

So Mama's words give us some information on how we got to Vienna. The above information was taken from scribbled notes from conversations with my mama. As far as I can determine, after a brief time in Vienna, we arrived in Germany. The experience of journaling the years of my adventure has aroused in me all the feelings that attend to sadness and gladness. The one statement that grips me more securely than any other is:

"GOD IS FAITHFUL!"

... a truth that is anchored in Scripture after Scripture in both the Old and New Testaments:

Therefore, know that He is your God, He is God, the Faithful God, Who keeps covenant and mercy for a thousand generations with those who love Him and keep His commandments.

Deuteronomy 7:9

Your mercy, O Lord, is in the heavens, and Your faithfulness reaches to the skies.

Psalm 35:6

O Lord God of Hosts, Who is mighty like you, O Lord? Your faithfulness also surrounds You.

Psalm 89:8

Forever, O Lord, Your word is settled in heaven. Your faithfulness endures to all generations.

Psalm 119:89-90

Through the Lord's mercies, we are not consumed, Because His compassions fail not. Great is Your faithfulness.

Lamentations 3:22-23

May the God of peace Himself sanctify you completely; and may your whole spirit, soul, and body be preserved blameless at the coming of our Lord Jesus Christ. He who calls you is faithful, who also will do it.

1 Thessalonians 5:23-24

Let us hold fast to the confession of our hope without wavering, for He who has promised is faithful.

Hebrews 10:23

Therefore, let those who suffer according to the will of God
commit their souls to Him in doing good,
as to a faithful Creator.

1 Peter 4:19

As you read this story, my prayer is that you will learn this one thing above all others:

GOD IS FAITHFUL!

Then I heard a loud voice saying in heaven,
"Now salvation, and strength, and the kingdom of our God,
and the power of His Christ have come,
for the accuser of our brethren,
who accused them before our God day and night,
has been cast down."
And they overcame him by the blood of the Lamb
and by the word of their testimony,
and they did not love their lives to the death.

Revelation 12:11

**This book represents both the existence of fierce warfare
and the protocol for overcoming.**

Chapter 1

Early Days and World War II

Before I formed you in the womb I knew you;
Before you were born I sanctified you;

Jeremiah 1:5a

Your eyes saw my substance, being yet unformed.
And in Your book they all were written,
The days fashioned for me,
When as yet there were none of them.

Psalm 139:16

My mother was a good storyteller. It may have taken some prodding to get her to begin to talk but when she started, truths from a dark period in our nation's history poured out like a tempestuous flood and my heart was stirred. Most of the stories she told me were about events and conditions that occurred and existed before I was born. Those stories are some of the most precious and intriguing I can remember, and I might say, at the same time, very disconcerting. My mother, who died in 2009, has certified most of the stories.

My husband, Jack, met my mother on our first visit to Germany together in 2005. It was to be followed by his second visit in 2008. By this time my mother was in a nursing home. Jack was impressed that she played the piano and had a heart for music. She was an accomplished musician that brought them more closely together since Jack had some training in that field. Happily, between them, it was love at first sight! She fell in love with him and he with her. He has, at his insistence, written a brief chapter about her entitled, One Solitary Woman. So this is my story, much of it from the sights and sounds seen and experienced, living around this great woman, my mama, Maria Dedeo Voss.

On our first visit to Germany, shortly after our wedding, Jack endeared mama to himself by learning the Aaronic Blessing in Numbers 6:24-26 and flawlessly quoting it to her during our first visit:

"Der HERR segne dich und behüte dich;
der HERR lasse sein Angesicht leuchten über dir und sei
dir gnädig;
der HERR hebe sein Angesicht über dich und gebe
dir Frieden."

"The Lord bless you and keep you;
The Lord cause His face to shine upon you and be gracious to
you.
The Lord lift up His countenance upon you and give you
peace."

She was so touched and impressed with this event that the next morning she asked him to do it again! He joyfully granted her request. For both of them, it was a never-to-be-forgotten experience, forging a bond between them that could not be broken.

My Home: The Beginning

I was born in Bratislava, Czechoslovakia during World War II to Karl and Maria Voss. My father was an accomplished and successful tailor who, in May of 1943, changed his last name from Vojtech, his Czechoslovakian name, to Voss, his German name. I have assumed, though never known for sure, that this name-change took place as a result of his desire to provide a better life for his family and to be more acceptable in Germany, the country that was methodically taking over all nearby territories. The decision to change his name proved very costly in that his birth family considered it a rejection on their part and all communication ceased. We were never to hear from them or of them from that time on.

His Czechoslovakian name would have been problematic as Germany viciously and violently took over a vast majority of the European countries. It may have looked like, for all practical purposes, that the whole world would soon be one very huge country under German rule.

This beautiful city of Bratislava is situated like a diamond split in two on either side of the Blue Danube. The German name for this city is Pressburg, and it is located near the state borders of Austria and Hungary. The city of Bratislava is widespread on both banks of the Danube River with a gigantic bridge connecting the city-center with the sprawling remainder of the city. It is now the capitol of Slovakia, which was, for centuries under the regimes of other stronger powers, such as the Magyars, the Austro-Hungarians, and of course the Czechs. Slovakia was part of Czechoslovakia until 1993, when it became a self-governed nation, the Slovak Republic.

Although Bratislava was flourishing, German troops were invading Central Europe and by 1939 the Czechoslovakian Republic was divided into two regions. The first region, the Czech, became a Nazi settlement region and Hitler, the insane leader of Nazi Germany, forced the Slovak politicians to come to a decision between two choices about Slovakia.

One choice was to divide Slovakia into many regions that would be part of Hungary, Poland, Moravia, and Bohemia. The second choice was the creation of a self-governed nation. The second decision prevailed, and a new nation was born! It took six years, more or less, to complete the implementation of the new country and this event proved to be a very important point in the history of the whole world. Bratislava then became the capital city of Slovakia. Unfortunately, the armed forces of the United States bombed the city at the end of the Second World War due to the fact that it was the capital city of a country that was Hitler's ally. After that in 1945 Bratislava merged into the Soviet Union. (http://www.bratislava.gr/en/index_history.htm)

It was into this violent, terrifying and turbulent world that a baby girl was born who would be saved from certain death by a random series of kindnesses of a nameless nurse. I was that baby girl! That story will be told later.

Toward the end of the war, allegedly in January of 1945, my father was drafted into the Waffen-SS to serve the "Fuehrer," Adolf Hitler. The literal translation for Waffen-SS is "Arms-SS." It was the combat arm of the *Schutzstaffel* or SS, an organ of the German Nazi Party. To be a member of this elite group one had to be trained in both attitude and action for violence and terror. This meant that these men were held in the rigid grip of a fanatical allegiance to the supreme leader, Hitler. They were the recognized expression of Hitler's reign while the dreaded "Gestapo" served as his secret police. The word "Fuehrer" in English is "Leader," a title used by Adolf Hitler to define his role of absolute authority in Germany's Third Reich (1933–1945). Few are alive today who have even a clue as to how near the world came to be ruled by an ingenious madman by the name of Adolph Hitler, later dubbed, simply "Hitler," who would become one of the most hated and malevolent names in human history. My father worked for this man and was forcefully devout to this maniac whose hate was so contagious, that no one who was associated with him seemed able to evade being infected, either as a victim on the receiving end of this maniacal hate or an obedient associate, enforcing his seemingly limitless evil.

While still in Czechoslovakia as an infant, I became severely ill with cholera and typhoid fever caused by the improper sanitation and lack of nourishment. After being hospitalized for several months, no improvement was in sight, and the doctors told my mother that there was nothing else they could do for me and that she needed to take me out of the hospital. The hospital needed the beds for wounded soldiers which made it necessary to discharge all patients that were not able to get well.

My mother, however, tried to reason with hospital personnel to keep me because she had no home. Our home in Bratislava was occupied by military troops, and she was hiding in the forest from the enemy with my older brother and sister and came to the hospital to check on me from time to time. She told the doctors her situation and pleaded with them to keep me. When a nurse working at that hospital overheard the conversation, she came to my mother and gave her the keys to her apartment and told her to take her other children and me and settle in her home. Additionally, she told her that the only way I even would have a chance of surviving would be for me to receive a blood transfusion and she offered to donate her own blood to keep me alive. My mother accepted her kind offer, saving my life.

Today I can say that when the physicians were out of options to save my life and left me to die, the "Great Physician," unbeknownst to me, had plans for me and in Job's words:

> *You have granted me life and favor,*
> *and Your care has preserved my spirit.*
>
> Job 10:12

God in His grace and mercy sent a nurse to give me a blood transfusion, saving my life and giving my little struggling family a roof over their heads. Sadly, I was never able to meet this nurse to thank her. Perhaps later I will find this nameless angel in a nurse's uniform and say, "Thank you!" for a random act of kindness without which I would never have lived past infancy.

According to my mother, at the war's end in 1945, my father became a prisoner of war (POW) of the American military and was held at Ebensee in Austria, formerly a Jewish concentration camp located at the southern tip of the Traun Lake approximately 75 kilometers southwest of Linz in Austria from 30 June until 12 September 1945. Camp Ebensee was established in November of 1943 and liberated by U.S. troops in May of 1945.

The SS had established the concentration camp to house some of the Jewish prisoners of war and use them as slave labor to build tunnels for armament storage near the town of Ebensee. It was part of the Mauthausen network. Due to the inhumane working and living conditions, Ebensee was recognized as one of the worst Nazi concentration camps for the high death rates of its prison population, approximately 20,000. The SS used several code names for it, such as Kalk, which means limestone; Kalksteinbergwerk, which means limestone mine as well as Zement, meaning cement, to conceal the true nature of the camp.

Together with the Mauthausen sub-camp of Gusen, Ebensee is considered to have been one of the most diabolical concentration camps ever built in the same category with the famed Dachau and Auschwitz.

The construction of the sub-camp began in late 1943, and the first 1,000 prisoners arrived in November 1943 from the main camp of Mauthausen and other Mauthausen sub-camps. The main purpose of Ebensee was to provide slave labor for the construction of the enormous underground tunnels to house armaments. (Information retrieved from http://www.jewishgen. org/forgottenCamps/Camps/EbenseeEng.html)

After the allied forces liberated Ebensee and released its Jewish prisoners, evidently the same facilities were used to house German soldiers as prisoners. Though my mother never shared information as to how my father got to Ebensee, I assumed that he was either working there or with a nearby German camp. She only mentioned that when she found out that my father was held there as a prisoner of the allied forces, she went to visit him. After arriving there, she was informed that my father could be released if she and he would be willing to promise to depart the country and deport to Germany, signing papers to that effect. My mother agreed with my father, and he was released.

In January of 1945 my mother, with her three children, departed Czechoslovakia for Vienna, where we were held as refugees until my father was released from Ebensee in September of 1945, located approximately 250 kilometers from Vienna, and sent to Germany where we joined him to begin life together again. This was how I came to West Germany where I was raised near Fulda.

A Further Word About Hitler

Before we leave this chapter, because the name "Hitler" appears in the title of this book, it seems appropriate that we observe some historical facts about this dark figure whose name and face dominated the world news during the years between 1933 and 1945, when in April of that year, he allegedly committed suicide with his wife, Eva Braun. This formally terminated the long reign of terror on the part of this ingenuous madman, holding the whole civilized world in its threatening grip.

While I am aware that many, if not most, of my readers have never heard the name of Hitler, it was my desire that my readers feel something of the tragic condition of the world into which I was born and share the priceless story of how one life was so blessed of God to such an extent that, perhaps some of the memories of suffering, injustices, atrocities and crimes of war could be blown away by breezes of hope. This is my story! It was my mother who, hoping against hopelessness, never lost her song and taught me to find that song. My love for Germany, the country of my childhood, still pleasures my heart. Now that I have lived in America for over fifty years, I happily return to Germany ever and again to commemorate with family our lives together and anticipate the years ahead with undying hope for a better world.

I make mention of Hitler here, first, because my father served as one of his elite troops during the last days of the war. He was assigned to extend the wishes of his leader who made it his aim to destroy everyone in his path whose presence might prevent his plans for world domination. Second, though I was born the year before Hitler died, many of the influences of this evil man were felt and seen in my early life, not only in the culture of my country but also through the behavior of my father. I had no idea of the magnitude of the shockwaves that awakened the people everywhere to the measure of the unspeakable tragedies that Hitler, this evil genius, brought into the world. The Hitler era will surely stand as one of the bloodiest seasons of all time, much of the bloodshed precipitated by Hitler by deliberate and shameless intent.

He is blamed for the methodical murder of at least six million Jews; some suggest that it is more likely to be as many as nine million. It is reported that, beyond this, as an added result of the wars that Hitler initiated, another forty million died with approximately twenty million of those from the Soviet Union. It should be remembered that, probably, as a result of the war in Europe, Japan chose to engage the United States with its surprise attack on Pearl Harbor on December 7, 1941. The magnitude of this war stuns the imagination as Hitler chose to attack Russia with millions of troops, further revealing his intentions of ruling the world.

It is today a sobering revelation to me that it was into Hitler's Germany that I came with my family and lived the first twenty years of my life after the war had ended. It is ironic also that my being a citizen of the United States was brought about by my marriage to an American soldier and my subsequent move to this country where I live to this day. It stuns my imagination even now as I look back on this season and realize how many factors God gathered together to bring me to this new land. I know now that it was none other than the providences of God that brought me to America.

It is my distinct privilege to invite you, the reader, to live the story with me with the prayer that your experience in the reading will be as pleasant, enjoyable and productive as mine has been in the telling.

Chapter 2

Childhood Memories

For behold, I create new heavens and a new earth; and the former shall not be remembered or come into mind.

Isaiah 65:17

I was not to know for many years that I was born and was living in one of the worst eras in the history of the world. From early memory, I had no standard by which to judge the quality of our lives or the lack thereof, or a grid to understand the kind of world to which I had opened my eyes. I didn't understand the stress and quiet desperation I felt in the atmosphere around me from my earliest memories, nor did I know why my father was dominated by hate or why he sought to instill in me a hatred for the Jews at an early age. I could not understand why, but tried to obey, though I constantly struggled with the thoughts that were stirring in me. But what did I know? I was just a child and a girl child at that? So many times even my gender was something the devil attacked through my father.

I was raised in a Catholic home without a Bible but with a keen sense of right and wrong, coupled with the fear of God encouraged by the Catholic faith.

My mother told me that my father had been a devout Catholic until he suffered the loss of everything of material value. These losses, coupled with the pain and sufferings all around him, caused him to renounce whatever faith he had and turn from God altogether.

I was raised by a mother who did the best she could with the circumstances at that time. My mother was a woman of beauty and wisdom and loved me unconditionally. My father had wanted a boy, and already had chosen a boy's name, so it seemed that he devalued me from birth. I was treated as if I was guilty of a deliberately rebellious choice to be a girl and my father never, to his death, let me forget it! It was the beginning of a struggle with my own identity that would last for many years. He made me feel like a loser as long as I can remember.

Surely he had to love me as I was his child, but his level of love did not give me a feeling of security and acceptance. He never affirmed me, never comforted me, never showed me any affection and never told me that he loved me. He always told me that I would never amount to anything and continuously compared me to my sister who was beautiful, tall and slender, whereas I was short and stocky. He constantly told me that I was fat and ugly. That ingrained a self-loathing that I battled for many years. It seems to me, as I recall my life as a child that my father went out of his way to let me know of his continuing displeasure with me. He lived a life of silence and isolation from his family, so I was never given reason to find solace in the word "father." I used the opportunity to isolate myself for protection and safety from my father. One of my favorite places as a child was in the darkest corner in the cellar where no one could find me, or a place under the weeping willow at the nearby cemetery. Though I never felt close to God, I cried out to Him in desperation, asking, "Why did you let me be born? I did not ask for this life. Just take me out of here somehow." I had no peace; I had no purpose to live.

I always spoke with a loud voice and was continuously reprimanded for it and was told to keep my voice down because "walls have ears," meaning that other people might be listening, and we may be overheard without our knowing it and picked up and questioned by the official secret state police, one of the sad leftovers from the Nazi era. This was a time when no one trusted anyone and everybody was suspicious of everybody else, constantly spreading lies about him or her.

At home, I was only allowed to speak when questions were

directed to me. I was not allowed to ask questions. As I became older and wanted to know information about the war, I was told that those questions were not to be asked.

Fortunately, I never bought into the lie of the fascist or Nazi philosophy. Hitler was never my leader. I never knew enough about him either to hate him or to love him. However, it wasn't until much later that I learned that he was behind the methodical massacre of millions of Jews. It might be simple to say, but it seemed that Hitler's struggle with his own identity led to catastrophic atrocities too heinous to comprehend or believe. Hitler had an uncommonly relentless ego best explained by one observation: demon possession! With driving passion, he ruled with maniacal plans and intentions to control the world. His plan was evil to the core.

These words were ascribed to Hitler over one of the gas chambers in Auschwitz:

"I want to raise a generation of young people
devoid of a conscience, imperious, relentless and cruel."

He left the marks of his evil intentions on everybody and everything he touched and my father was unwittingly a part of Hitler's evil plans, serving (probably against his will) his supreme commander, Hitler, as a member of the feared and violent "Waffen-SS," Hitler's body guards, the Nazi enforcers. Thus my own life was touched by the influence of an unloving father and the culture of a notoriously evil system, the Third "Reich" (German word for "kingdom" or "empire")!

My parents eventually rented a two-room apartment in a very small village in West Germany near the border that divided the east from the west. The village consisted of only seven houses. Many of the homeowners were related to each other and considered us to be "Zigeuner," which in the English language could be translated as "gypsies" and was used in a derogatory way because of its negative and stereotypical associations. We were treated with isolation, suspicion, and disdain.

The apartment was upstairs and accessible only from the back of the house through the courtyard which was guarded by a dog that was on a long free roaming chain able to reach every person entering. I was very much afraid of this dog because he was not friendly to us at all, which contributed to me not wanting to go home. The entrance door to the apartment consisted of thin plywood and did not provide much shelter in winter during freezing temperatures. There were times that we could not open the door because of heavy snow during the night and had to open it inch by inch, first with a spoon and then with a shovel.

One of the rooms served as a kitchen and family room, the other as our bedroom in which we had two beds and one cot. My parents slept in one of the beds, my sister and I in the other. I might mention that these were no Queen or King sized beds in those days. They were just regular size beds. My older brother had to sleep on the cot. Because we did not have a bathroom in our apartment, we used a portable aluminum bathtub in which we bathed once a week, and that on Saturdays. In order to have some privacy while bathing, my father drove a hook into two opposite walls of the apartment to which he attached a string from one wall to the other and hung sheets over them to separate the kitchen area from the family room. We had to place the tub on the kitchen floor while my mama heated water on the stove because we did not have hot running water and poured it into the bathtub to allow us to have warm water for bathing. Because I was the youngest, I had to wait until after my brother and sister had taken their bath before I could take mine, and that in the same water. It was in that environment that I grew up as a child.

I remember that my sister and I continuously fought over the bed covers to stay warm and kicked each other in the shins to keep from getting too close to each other. We used to fight like cat and dog, and because I was the younger one, I always had to sleep next to the wall and crawl over her to get into or out of bed, which in itself was enough reason to fight, and fight we did. I remember one situation where I had become so angry with my sister that I used a large cast iron skillet to hit her on the head. My mother was visiting with the tenant below our apartment and must have heard all the ruckus from above. The next thing I remembered was that my mother stood between us just when I was swinging that heavy skillet. It was only by the grace of God that I did not hit her on the head with it and was able to turn my arm moving the skillet away from her. I still thank God for His intervention during that moment.

During the winter months, when the temperature dropped to freezing and below, glistening frost built up on the wallpaper on my side of the bed. My favorite pastime was to write on the wall with my fingers and watch the frost melt.

While I was still a small child, my father would yell at me and tell me that I was no good for anything, always finding fault in me, telling me that I was like the hunchback of Notre Dame with my shoulders slouched or like the ugly duckling. According to him, my lips were too big, my neck was too short, and so on. As a result of these constant negative remarks, I always felt like the 'black sheep' of the family, being made to feel like an outcast and treated with disdain by my father and my sister and as a result I had developed a low self-esteem, a lack of self-worth, and became very insecure. I wondered if my father even saw one redeeming feature in my whole person.

I never felt comfortable in my father's presence and was even afraid to be with him by myself. Every opportunity I had, I went to the farm near our home that had cows, horses, pigs and other animals. The owner of that farm was a very compassionate man and knew our family's situation. He also knew that I had much rather spend my time on his farm than at home. As a result, he always told my father that he needed me to watch his cows in the meadows so they would not cross the fence into the adjacent farmer's land. I think he must have taken a liking to me and felt sorry for me. This thoughtful farmer gave me feelings of safety and acceptance that my father had denied me. So I happily enjoyed milking the cows, feeding the pigs, cleaning the stalls or whatever else needed to be done on the farm. It was payment enough for me just to escape the constant rejection of my father at home. I suppose that my time on the farm with the livestock and all would make me somewhat of a cowgirl or ranch hand today. Without my knowledge, God might have been preparing me to be the wife of a country boy from Texas (a story to come later)!

My dad was a tailor by trade, and, I might say, a very good one. As a matter of fact, he was so good that every stitch had to be perfect. Every buttonhole was made by hand and had to be flawless. To tell the truth, my father was a perfectionist in everything he did. The inevitable downside of his perfectionism was that he expected everybody around him to be perfect as well. Thus, no one could meet his expectations of perfection. When we did not and could not measure up to his perfect standards, he made sure to let us know in no uncertain terms that there was hell to pay. I was never the brightest candle on the Christmas tree and, looking back, I did some amazingly dumb things. In Germany, we used to attach real candles to the Christmas tree and then light them in the evenings while singing Christmas songs. One evening I was allowed to light the candles on the tree. I was very young and short for my age and had to get a chair to reach each candle on the top part of the tree, so I started at the bottom where it was most convenient for me. Instead of teaching me to start lighting the candles at the top and work downward because of the possible danger of getting burned, my father became outraged and told me how stupid I was to start at the bottom when everybody knows you start at the top! Like I said, I was very young and not very bright. Anyway, that was the last we saw of my father during that particular Christmas season.

As a result of that little episode, my father, as he often did after a moment of anger or outburst, retreated to the bedroom of our two-room apartment and did not come out until after New Years. My mama had to bring him food and because we had no bathroom in our apartment he used a "potty" which my mama had to take downstairs to the "outhouse" to empty. There were several other occasions when he acted that way, and there were days and sometimes even weeks during which he would not speak to anyone, not even my mama who had to work for him. Because of that one event above when my father stepped into his silent treatment because of my 'stupidity', I always assumed that my being there was the reason for my father's anger and silence.

All we could do during those times was whisper to each other in the adjacent room lest he might suddenly appear, furious and enraged and beat us all unmercifully. During these times of his silent treatment, often turning violent, he would not give my mama money to buy groceries. That's when I would go to the farmer's house and ask whether I could milk the cows, clean the stalls or do whatever I could for a slice of bread for myself and my mama, brother and sister.

During my school years I was never allowed to invite friends to our house nor was I ever allowed to go to other children's homes. For you to be able to understand why I could not keep friends, I will give you one example: I am sure you are familiar with the saying "children will be children." And so, one day after school, a girl grabbed my book bag and ran off with it. I started to run after her, but I knew by the time I would arrive at her home I would be late in getting to my home and would be punished. So I turned around and went home without my book bag. After I arrived, my father asked me where I had been. I had trouble on all sides and could not win for losing. When I explained to him what happened and asked him whether I could get my books from the girl's home in order to do my homework, he would not allow it. After about two hours the neighbor living below us came up and asked whether I could come downstairs. She mentioned that a girl was asking for me. My father did not allow me to go but went himself instead. The next day I was told that he slapped her face for snatching my book bag. Situations like this one were not conducive to making or keeping friends. The sad result was that I never had any friends during all my childhood years; that meant no birthday party invitations and no slumber parties.

On one occasion, when I was at home by myself with my father, I all of a sudden felt something in my back causing me much pain while trying to prepare dinner. My father, without warning, had thrown one of his large industrial sized cone of yarn and deliberately aimed it at my back! My crime? Standing with my legs in a relaxed position with one foot on top of the other rather than in "attention" mode he demanded. This was a playback from his days as one of Hitler's "goons" when they stamped their feet and snapped their heels. That episode added to my fears of being at home alone with him.

To be fair to my father, I must say that he was not all bad, in fact, he was such an excellent tailor that as a result of his excellence he was asked to move his tailor shop closer to town so that he would be nearer to his clientele. He rented a room in a small town approximately two kilometers from where we lived.

There were times when he would not come home for days or even weeks. That meant that when our limited food supply ran out, we were simply without anything to eat. We actually were thankful just for a slice of bread and a cup of water. On some of those occasions, when we were hungry, we would walk to my father's shop to ask him for a slice of bread. At that time bread was sold in bakeries as loaves and was not cut into slices to keep its freshness longer. I remember on one occasion watching my dad cutting off a real thin slice with his knife and then spread baking margarine on it (the kind that sticks to your gums, similar to baking lard) while he cut himself a slice much thicker and spread it with butter. This memory sticks out so much in my mind and reinforced the idea that we, especially I, would never come first in his life.

As I remember these events, I recall one cold winter day when my father took a "nap" on his large tailoring table in the living room where I was doing my homework. The sound of the turning of the page in my notebook awakened him from his nap, and he ordered me to do my homework outside our apartment on the hall staircase to keep from being disturbed. I dutifully obeyed and finished my homework with gloves on to keep my fingers from freezing. Have you ever tried to write with gloves? During those days the hallways were not built with heaters.

My mother had to walk daily these two kilometers through rain, snow or shine to get to my father's shop. One day, when I was able to accompany her, a thunderstorm came out of nowhere, and a lightning bolt struck behind us. The sound and the brightness of that strike scared me out of my wits. I turned around and saw a man lying on the street a few meters away. Evidently, that lightning bolt had struck him. I cannot recall what we did, but from that time for years I was terrified every time a thunderstorm came. That fear may have been the result of my thinking that it could have struck me, and the next one may be for me. When I saw that, I thought about how on that day a few yards made the difference between life and death.

Most of the time my siblings and I were left to ourselves, but we had definite chores that had to be done. We had to scrub the floors on our hands and knees and then wax it and buff it the same way. We had to chop wood with the ax for our wood stove to be able to cook and stay warm in the winter. On one occasion when my older brother was swinging his ax to split a huge wooden block, I had the urge to give him a big hug but did not realize that he had the ax in his hand and ready to swing. It was truly a miracle that he did not split my head in two but only cut my eyebrow, barely missing the eye. I truly believe that God being Omniscient sent His angels in advance to guide my steps and protect me from a serious calamity. Could it be that He had a purpose for my life, and I was completely unaware of it? I believe that to be so!

We had no time to be bored. I believe boredom allows the mind to run free, and when the mind runs free, it usually is in the direction of darkness and eventual disaster. That was not a problem at our busy house!

I remember those times well when we made toast on top of the stove, then rubbed it with garlic, a habit I still enjoy repeating. I seemed to be hungry all the time, and I was never choosy about food. For our family, it was pure survival. We did not have any money. All too often my mother went to the butcher shop and asked for the bones that had been stripped of their meat and ready to be discarded by the butcher. She then would boil these bones with whatever little leftover meat there may have been to make some kind of broth and added barley to it. To this day I do not like barley. She also added some parsley or chives that she had planted in a little corner of soil in the landlord's garden for additional nourishment.

My mother was an amazing woman. She knew exactly what plants growing in the wild were rich in nourishment to keep us healthy in the midst of poverty. She could always fix something to eat out of virtually "nothing," such as stinging nettle spinach. She sent us out to gather these wild growing stinging nettles along highways. Needless to say, as the name reveals, coming in touch with fresh nettle will sting any skin it comes into contact with, causing itchy, burning welts like fire ants. We, therefore, took extra caution and wore long pants, boots, long sleeves and gloves to gather them. That was the only kind of spinach I knew as a child. Additionally, we were sent to the woods to gather "Pfifferlinge" which are Chanterelle mushrooms, "Steinpilze" which are Boletus_edulis and "Wiesenchampignons," also known as Field mushrooms, which my mother made into wonderfully tasting dishes. Additionally, we had to gather "Spitzwegerich" for which the American name is "Ripwort"—a scary sounding name—that grew wild along the highway. Mom also prepared homemade cough syrup from it, which, as I remember, was rather tasty. For the most part, however, I do not recall ever having seen a doctor during all my childhood years except when once I had swallowed a fish bone, and it was stuck in my throat crosswise, and my mom had to get a doctor to come to the house and remove the bone. During those days, doctors made house calls. How convenient!

During the days of my upbringing, it was unthinkable for us to dress in any type of torn clothing. Therefore, we learned to darn our socks when they had holes in them and to repair any type of clothing. I always wore "hand-me-downs." New clothing was never part of my experience or my vocabulary.

After a couple of years, the family moved to town where my father had his tailor shop. This was to keep my mom from having to walk so far every day to work for him. Our new apartment still consisted of only two rooms, one a family room that had a small corner as a kitchen, a dining room table, a big sewing machine and a large table on which my father did all his measurements and suit or dress pattern preparations. The other room was a bedroom in which the whole family slept. The apartment did not have a bathroom. The minute nature called we had to start heading down the stairs, along a long hallway, through the garden that led to a barn. Then we had to go through the barn out the back, walk up a slight hill and there we finally reached the "outhouse," come rain or shine, snow or ice. My sister and I again had to share the same bed, and my brother had to sleep on a cot that was positioned at the foot of our bed.

One day my father sent my sister to get milk from the farmer's house in the other village, and I went with her because I did not want to stay at home by myself with my father. Instead of going around the house through the courtyard to enter at the front door, we took a shortcut and entered from the back of the house through the cow barn that was separated from the living quarters by a huge sliding door. As I pulled the door shut, my finger got stuck between the door and the wall, and I smashed my finger so hard that it was bleeding profusely and, I might add, hurting severely. When we got back home, I received a severe beating because I left without his permission and for being, as my father observed, so "stupid and not watching what I was doing," without a single word of sympathy for my pain!

Because of all my negative experiences, I do not have many good memories of my childhood. When, as a child, I asked my mother why my father did not love me, she always told me that it was my imagination. But over the years I became more and more convinced that my father not only did not love me but also counted me of little or no value to him. After all, he wanted a boy, and I was a girl. I was not to forget this, and he saw to it by giving me a boy's name and reminded me that I would move out the day I turned twenty-one years of age. This was the legal age at which parents were no longer responsible for their children. My father always told me that I would never amount to anything. I could not please my father, no matter what I tried to do.

When twelve years later my mother became pregnant with my younger brother, my father told her that he would buy her a washing machine if she would birth him a boy. Guess what? He was a boy, but my father never bought her that washing machine. Another memory was born to remind me of my father's pitiful life!

On my sixteenth birthday, I thought I would try to use lipstick. When my father saw me, he told me that I looked like a whore, confiscated my lipstick and made me wash it off. Now I need to mention that he had no problem with my sister wearing lipstick when she put it on, and she was, in his word, beautiful. If this all sounds rather unfair to my father, my final word about him will explain my present feelings of peace.

On another occasion, after my seventeenth birthday, a young man wanted to take me to a movie, and I asked my dad for permission to go. He was in a pretty good mood that day and actually gave his permission. On the day when the young man came to pick me up, my father changed his mind and told me I could not go anywhere. In fact, I could not even go downstairs to tell the young man that I was no longer allowed to go and had to let him stand outside the house until he got tired of waiting and left.

Based on situations like those above, I disliked my father more and more and wanted to run away from home. However, I had one problem: there was no place to go! My thoughts were: "What will I eat, where will I sleep, what will I wear?" Does that sound familiar? Doesn't the Bible say that these things dominate the thoughts of unbelievers? And yes, I was an unbeliever!

I do not remember how long we lived in that particular apartment before we moved to another one in that same town. There we still had only two rooms, but at least we did not have to go outside to use the bathroom. Now we only had to go to the downstairs hall that contained an outhouse with a pit latrine made out of wood within the building. It was not heated and very cold in the winter. When the wind blew, you could feel it. I would like to say we froze our little tails off.

Although my parents instilled in us children good character, honor, and integrity, we were never taught biblical principles. We did not even own a Bible, and God was never among the subjects we were allowed to discuss. We were Catholic by name, but not really Christian in the truest and strictest sense of the word. The school I attended had religion as one of the mandatory subjects for Catholics and Protestants. I remember that in our class we had one girl who was a Jehovah's Witness and she was allowed to go home during that hour. That made me wish I was a Jehovah's Witness so that I could skip that hour. What I do remember from these hours of study on religion was that Jesus was the Son of God who came to earth to die on a cross for my sins. Then He was buried, raised again on the third day and ascended into heaven. While I believed that these were valid facts, I was not encouraged toward a personal experience with Jesus Christ. I had been baptized into the Catholic faith when I was three days old and was told that I would eventually go to heaven when I died after spending some time in purgatory. According to Catholic Church doctrine, Purgatory is an intermediate state after physical death in which those, destined for heaven, would undergo purification, so as to achieve the holiness necessary to enter the joys of heaven. The length of time in purgatory depended on the severity of our sins. It may sound strange, but I had no desire to go to heaven because I equated heaven as the place where God the Father lived. My silent assumption was that this God was a father not unlike my own father, and I was not interested in a relationship with him. I saw God as a harsh authoritarian figure to be feared, rigidly obeyed and difficult to please. I wanted a father who loved me; one I could honor, cherish and yes, love!

My father was raised in the Catholic faith but turned away from that belief. He seemed indifferent and at times even hostile when the word "God" was mentioned. I often heard him say that there could be no God such as to allow us to lose all our earthly belongings and endure all the sufferings during the war. I am sorry to say that my father blamed God for much of his failure and misfortune. Now it seems a strange paradox that, though to my father there was no God, yet he hated him. Go figure! My question was, "How can anyone hate something or someone that does not exist?"

My mother, on the other hand, was a believer in God and tried to attend church on Sunday with us as often as she could. But I do remember, more often than not, my father actually forbidding her and us children to go to church. One of the reasons given was that the excessive walking would wear down the soles of our shoes, as we had to walk more than two kilometers each way. That would eventually require a shoe repair or even a new pair of shoes. I remember little things like this that increased my dislike for my father and decreased my hope for a better life.

Prior to my graduation from school, I applied for a job at the local "Deutsche Bundespost," a civil service job with the Post Office. Because there were no vacancies, they suggested I send my application to the postal headquarters in Frankfurt. Here I saw an opportunity to get away from home legally and still be able to eat and have a roof over my head. It was not long after I submitted my application that I received acceptance papers that had to be signed by my father. I thought surely he would sign them, especially since he could get me out of the house before reaching twenty-one. I was supposed to have sent the paperwork back within three weeks to start employment immediately upon my graduation. When I approached my father, he refused to sign the papers. I was crushed. This was in the spring of the year. At Christmas that year my father asked me for the papers and said that he would sign them as my Christmas present. I complained to my mom because it was way past the deadline that the postal authorities had set. My mother, however, told me to let my father sign the papers and instructed me to mail them right away. Shortly after I submitted the papers I received instructions as to when and where to report in Frankfurt. I was informed that I would live in a dormitory where I would have a curfew and would be required to sign in every night by ten PM because I was not yet eighteen years of age. Between the ages of eighteen and twenty-one, I would have to sign in no later than midnight.

When it was time to leave home, my father took me to the train station and the last words he said, while the train was moving were, and I quote: "Denke nur nicht dass Du einen roten Pfennig von mir bekommen wirst!" ("Don't even think that you will get one red cent from me!") When I heard that I thought to myself that I had rather die than ask him for anything. Those words sealed my certainty as to my father's lack of love for me and left me with little hope that I would ever have a father's approval.

Shortly after I went to work in Frankfurt, my family moved north to Westphalia to a small town about which I knew nothing. For my first vacation, I took a train to spend that week with my family. My father picked me up from the train station, and we walked to the two-story house where they now lived on the upper floor. He was very kind and showed me every room, the kitchen, the living room and three bedrooms, one for my parents, one for my two brothers and the other for my sister. Now I naturally assumed that I would sleep in my sister's room. However, it had only one bed in it, and she made it very clear that I was not going to sleep in her room. Sure enough, there was no room for me, and I slept in the living room on the floor during that entire week.

As children and even into early adulthood our relationship was never very close, and we never did things together that sisters normally would do. On the contrary, we had continuous conflicts. This relationship, however, began to change over the years. On one occasion, the celebration of her seventieth birthday, I invited her to visit me in Florida with the intent of gifting her with a flight to Hawaii. She was so overcome with gratitude and apologized to me for having pushed me off our kitchen bench when we were children. During that incident, I had injured my shoulder but always thought that it was the result of my alleged clumsiness. So, after almost six decades my sister experienced remorse for how she had treated me as a child. We are able now to relate happily as loving sisters and best friends.

During the years with my father, I had felt like an outsider even with my own family. Thus I was very confused when my father suggested that I make a request for a job transfer from my current location in Frankfurt to where they now lived. I had a hard time with that because I felt no welcome at home on that prior visit. I surely did not want to sleep on the floor over a lengthy period of time. I later found out that my father's suggestion that I come back home was not based on his change of heart to love me, but to have me pay a monthly rent. My heart was broken again!

Needless to say, for my next vacation a year later I did not go home but went to visit the family in that small village with seven houses that had a guesthouse and the farm with the cows, horses, and pigs. One late afternoon during that week a young American soldier stopped in for a coke from his fishing trip on which he had caught quite a few trout. He was assigned to the 14th Armored Cavalry Regiment stationed in Downs Barracks in Fulda and mostly served on the border to East Germany, guarding freedom's frontier to include the Fulda Gap. His barracks were approximately six miles from where I spent the week. While there, he came back every day, and soon we exchanged telephone numbers. After I returned to Frankfurt for work, he surprised me one weekend when he showed up at the dormitory where I lived.

Without going into much detail, that soldier and I fell in love and later married. Prior to our marriage he and I went to visit my family to receive their blessing for our wedding. Several months after we were married, the military transferred my husband to the United States where we made our home and raised three children.

I would soon begin life in a whole new world whose language and culture would be totally strange to me. The issues to be faced would be drastic. The challenges to be met would be fierce. The changes that demanded attention would be insurmountable. But the possibilities and promises would be incomprehensible!

Chapter 3

Early Years in America: Extreme Culture Shock!

*I would have lost heart, unless I had believed that I would
see the goodness of the Lord in the land of the living. Wait
on the Lord; be of good courage, and He shall strengthen
your heart; Wait, I say, on the Lord!*

Psalm 27:13-14

A Whole New World

After several hours of flying, we started descending into the
Charleston, South Carolina airport when my ears started to hurt
and the pain worsened as the plane kept descending. I did not
realize unequal pressures that developed on either side of the
eardrum as the plane was prepared for landing caused this pain.
This being my first time to experience air travel, I had no clue as
to what was happening. I did not know what to do except suffer
excruciating pain until the plane finally landed. This experience
took away much of the excitement and joy I had felt earlier, and
for the next six months, I suffered from severe earaches. Before
we exited the plane, I noticed that it was raining outside and
tried to get my coat out of my carry-on bag, assuming that it
would be cool outside as it normally was in Germany when it
rained. But the moment I got out of the plane, instead of being
introduced to cool air I experienced the highest humidity that I
had ever witnessed. Needless to say, I did not need my coat.

From Charleston, we took a bus to Georgia to meet my new
family, my in-laws who lived in South Georgia. After a few days
trying to get acclimatized, we purchased a used car and drove to

Columbus, Georgia where my husband had to report to his new duty station at Fort Benning. There in Columbus we rented a duplex in what turned out to be a rather unsafe neighborhood with break-ins and thefts almost every time we left the home. This was completely new to me, to come home to find my house in disarray and items missing. Whoever had entered ransacked every drawer and closet and broke the piggy bank, taking all the money I had been saving for my little baby boy, Gene. I had started to save money for him, and all the money was gone. After a couple of times, I decided to leave the bedroom lights on to indicate that someone was at home. But guess what? You guessed right! When we came home, someone was inside and ran out the back door. That scared me so much that I no longer wanted to live there and wanted to go back to Germany. This would be a feeling recurring many times over the next months. We then looked for a different place to live, this time further out in Alabama. This house was a wooden structure, and we could feel the wind blowing between the wooden boards. I had never lived in a home like that before, and frankly, our chicken coupes in Germany were more solidly built than this house. To keep warm inside the house during the winter, I wore my snow boots and a heavy sweater. I put the playpen in front of the gas heater with my son in it so that he could be warm as well. I used my German down-feather pillow that I had brought from Germany to cover him up. It was almost the size of the playpen and large enough. However, I made it work, but I still wanted to go back home to Germany!

Approximately four months after we arrived in Georgia, my husband had to report to Lawson Army Airfield at Fort Benning early one morning for deployment on a secret mission. He was not permitted to tell me where he was going or for how long he would be gone. I remember that I had a dental appointment that morning and tried to stop by at the airfield to see him before he left; however, just before I got there I saw the plane take off.

Here we were, so close and yet so far! I do not recall how long it was before he returned home, but I found out in the meanwhile that he was deployed to the Congo to rescue nuns that were taken hostage by the rebel leader and were forced into hard labor with numerous atrocities having been reported by news agencies all over the world. Here I was, not quite four months in a new country and a strange culture with a small baby, surroundings unknown to me, and not understanding the language.

Now Christmas came around, and I was accustomed to having a fresh tree from the forest, which we decorated with clip-on candleholders and real white wax candles placed in them. In the evenings we would sit around the tree with a hot cup of cocoa, singing Christmas songs. But now the candleholders were not available, so my husband purchased the strings of colorful electric lights. To me these were not Christmas tree lights; they seemed more like carnival lights. To top it off, the people I became acquainted with were drinking and celebrating like we did in Germany during 'Fasching', the week of partying leading up to Mardi Gras. Two cultures were in conflict, and I felt out of place in the present one.

Other reasons I was so unhappy and depressed was the heat and humidity. I wanted snow. For me, it was not Christmas without it. Who had ever heard of walking around in shorts on Christmas Day, especially in front of the Christmas tree? Frankly, I was very homesick and had the idea that the only way to cure this disease was to go back to Germany. Another thing happened that worsened the disease.

One particular morning, about forty-five minutes after my husband had gone to work, I received a phone call and thought it was he, especially at 5:30 in the morning. When I answered the call, a female voice said: "Why don't you go back to Krautland where you belong?" I was shocked, especially since I had expected my husband to be on the other end of the receiver that early in the morning, and I asked who was talking. I received the same answer: "Why don't you go back to 'Krautland' where you belong." When I asked who is this, the caller immediately hung up the receiver. I had never heard that expression before, and when I told my husband, he told me that some Americans called German people "Krauts" as a derogatory term for a German, expressing contempt or disapproval. Do I need to tell you what I told my husband? You guessed it—I want to go back home to Germany! That phrase, "I want to go home" would be heard again and again until, in my husband's mind, he had heard it enough. I am sure you've heard the expression, "the straw that broke the camel's back." Well, one day I said it again, and that was it for my husband. He simply had his fill and would hear no more. He then made a shocking proposition, "If you want to go back to Germany, you may go but our son is staying here with me." You may be sure that he never heard that word from me again, though I may have thought it many times! Well, I am still here and after living here for more than half a century, I would not want to live permanently anywhere else. Oh, I like to go back to Germany once in a while to visit family and experience Christmas the way it used to be as a child with snow and a Christmas tree with white candles. But even that has changed now. Some things we can never go back to because inevitable changes constantly take place, and nothing is the way it used to be. One thing is forever settled. I am not going back to the "good old days!" Principally because they simply do not exist.

After a few months, we decided to buy a home closer to Fort Benning, which was located in South Columbus, a very nice neighborhood at that time. It had a fenced-in yard that I liked in order to let my little boy play outside, as he got older. The families living in this neighborhood were mostly military which I saw as a plus because they understood the military lifestyle. There was one fly in the ointment: One of our next-door neighbors disliked me merely because I was a German. There was nothing I could do to defend being what and who I was. So I was sentenced to her sneering stares and stark silence when I tried to speak to her. Not that she said anything insulting to me, but her silence was deafening, and that certain look on her face was enough to make me want to remove myself from her presence when I walked outside while she talked with my husband at the fence. She had many words for him but not one word for me!

If you ever were in the military, you will understand that it is a different culture than the civilian population. As a Noncommissioned Officer in the Army, my husband was more absent than present due to weekly or sometimes monthly training and also frequent deployments. Eventually, we accepted this lifestyle as a norm much to my chagrin. All this was happening while our family was rapidly growing.

We had two more children in as many years, and we three became five! This added to the rigors of multiple adjustments and really took a toll on me. When the youngest was six weeks old, as a matter of fact on the day of my six-week check up, my husband was deployed to Vietnam, leaving almost immediately. I was left with a six-week-old son, a one-year-old daughter and a two-and-one-half-year-old son while still trying to learn the language. As we say in America "My plate was quite full and getting fuller!"

I always like to say it is a wonder that my children did not die from "food poisoning" as I did not know what to give them to eat. I was unable to understand the labels on the baby food jars and I had to rely on others to tell me what was good for my children to eat and what was not. Today I say it was by the grace of God that my children remained healthy and robust!

A Quick Lesson on Culture

On one hot summer afternoon, I drove with my children to my husband's uncle's house about eleven miles away when after six miles the car stalled at a major intersection and would not start again. What was I to do? Here I was with three small children and no help. I had no phone, no way to call for help. I could not sit in the car with my children as the temperature was extremely hot. All I could do is get out of the car, carry two of them and asking the two-and-one-half-year-old son to walk beside me, holding on tightly to my slacks and walk toward my destination, approximately five miles. After a short distance, a car pulled over and a total stranger asked me whether he could give me a ride. I was overwhelmed with fear based on all the stories I heard on the news about people being abducted. But what choice did I have? I could not walk five miles holding two children in my arms and expect the other one to walk that distance. I had no choice but to say a quick prayer asking God to convict that man to take us to my uncle's house and get in that car. Thankfully he brought us to the place I asked him to take us and immediately left. When I entered the uncle's house, he asked me who that was in the car, and I told him my situation in the only English language I knew, and said: "I am so pissed off, my car is at that main intersection five miles down the road and this young man offered to give us a ride and bring us here." The uncle looked strangely, and kind of embarrassingly to his visitor, then to his wife, and they all looked at me. Then the uncle proceeded to tell me that I should not get in the car with strangers, and I was lucky that he brought us here. How well did I know that! Immediately after that the visitor excused himself and left. Well, just then I received a lesson of the English language and was told that he, my husband's uncle, knew that I did not know any better, but that the proper word was "perturbed," and by the way, that was our pastor.

I felt bad, but as he said, I did not know any better. I learned English from what I heard, being around soldiers. I know not all of them used that kind of language, but that was the environment I was around at that time. This was not the last time something like this happened, but I was determined to be more careful to express anger or frustration than before!

As I mentioned earlier, the neighborhood we lived in consisted mostly of military families because it was near the entrance of the military base. When the war in Vietnam was well advancing, most of the soldiers from our neighborhood were sent to Vietnam. Quite often we saw military cars with two men in uniform driving into our neighborhood. To us, that meant bad news, as one of these soldiers was a chaplain and the other a Notification officer and they were on their way to notify a spouse of her husband's death. We always prayed that they wouldn't stop at our house and also prayed for those who were the recipients of the bad news.

During the Vietnam era, the military did not have any support groups for the spouses and families that were left behind as they do now. At that time the saying was "If the military wanted the soldier to have a family they would have issued him one." This thinking, however, began to change with the establishment of the first Family Advocacy Program in 1981, which was followed by the first Army Family Symposium in the same year.

To Hell and Back

It is said that war is hell. I agree that war is that and more to every person who, in any way is connected to the warrior. Vietnam was a special version of hell. All these problems had to be faced sooner than I suspicioned. After my husband was informed that Vietnam was his next assignment, I was left to care, not only for the children but also the details of all the family business. I joined the other wives in the struggles with loneliness and fear that husbands and fathers might never come home, a dark cloud that constantly hung over our neighborhood. This meant that we were left to struggle with our own issues and try to take care of ourselves as best we could as our husbands were sent to fight in Vietnam.

I recall one incident in which I had to go to the store and take all three children with me because I did not have a babysitter. When I walked into the store people commented that I should just leave my children at home instead of dragging them in here. But I had no choice - I could not afford a babysitter. My husband left me with very little money in the form of a monthly allotment and had most of his money sent to him in Vietnam. The next time I had to go to the store just to get milk, I parked the car directly in front of the store while leaving my few-week-old youngest son in the car in his infant seat on the front passenger seat. The distance from the car to the front door was approximately five feet. During my few minute absence that poor child tried to turn over for the first time in his life, and I found him on the floorboard, face down, strapped in the baby carrier. Car seats as we know them today were not available at that time. I wanted to die! I was so ashamed, what a horrible mother I was! I felt so sorry for my son. But I can tell you this - from then on I took all my children with me wherever I went and no longer cared about the peoples' opinions! My concern for my children far outweighed what my neighbors or anyone else thought.

I did not share that incident with my husband when I wrote him because I figured that my problems were nothing compared to what he had to endure in combat. I had little contact with my husband while he was deployed. It was weeks and sometimes months between letters and I never really knew if he was dead or alive because of the lack of communication. There were no phone calls, no e-mails, no Skype, no text messaging or Facebook. I never really knew what was happening to my husband.

Then came a time, after my husband was gone for about six months, that I did not receive any mail from him for a very long time and became concerned and worried that something might have happened to him. Then one day I received a letter addressed to me with unfamiliar handwriting and postmarked in Vietnam. I was afraid to open it and called my husband's uncle who had retired from the military. He told me if anything serious would have happened to my husband they would have sent someone to my door. That gave me a little comfort and so I opened the letter, hands still shaking. It contained a note and the pictures of our children and a money order that I had sent to my husband. The note read as follows: "Dear Mrs. McDonald, these pictures and the money order where found in a trash can and given to me. There is no one here by that name. Therefore, I am returning them to you."

I could not believe what I was reading, and I was scared that something had really happened to my husband. My imaginations went wild adding to the experience of the myriad of aftershocks in a strange new culture.

That very evening I turned on the Evening News to find out what the News had to say about Vietnam. The first information was that enemy forces attacked Phu Loi, and the casualties were heavy. When I heard that, it seemed as if my heart had stopped beating. I felt numb because my husband was stationed in that village and I was afraid he might have been one of the casualties, and I might never see him again. What could I do? The only option I had was to wait.

After more than two weeks I received a letter from my husband informing me that he had been hospitalized as a result of injuries sustained and therefore was not able to write me. He had, without my knowledge, requested that I not be notified in case of injuries, only in case of death. In that letter, he also informed me that while on his reconnaissance patrols as a scout he usually checked on his buddy who was stationed in a village nearby to chat with and encourage him. On this particular day as he entered the village the soldiers who usually greeted and welcomed him now scurried away, leaving my husband to suspicion that something was not right. As he tried to find out, he was told that his buddy was hit by a hand grenade and blown to pieces!

I could sense the pain of my husband in that letter, and I grieved for him as well as for that soldier's wife. Prior to his and my husband's departure to Vietnam that soldier and his wife were at our house for a farewell party. While we were having a nice evening, that soldier's wife asked her husband whether he would be wearing a bulletproof vest while in Vietnam. I remember his answer so clearly as if he said it yesterday. His reply was, "I would look kind of foolish with a bullet-proof vest behind the bar!" Today this soldier's name is one of the 58,272 names on the Vietnam Veterans Memorial in Washington, DC according to "thewall-usa.com" website.

Shattered Hopes and Dreams

Turn Yourself to me, and have mercy on me,
for I am desolate and afflicted.
The troubles of my heart are enlarged;
bring me out of my distresses.

Psalm 25:16-17

It was to be a great day in our lives. Our husband and father was coming home after more than a year of separation. He called me from the New York airport and told me that he would arrive the next day and would call me with the time of arrival. I was very excited, yet nervous. What would he look like? How did the stress of combat affect him? How will the children receive their father they don't really know? So many questions ran through my mind. I did not know what to expect.

When that day of my husband's return from Vietnam had finally arrived, and I was able to have him back home with us, one of the neighbors from two blocks down the street, whose husband was still in Vietnam, saw us arriving and came over within the hour with a "six-pack" of beer as a welcome gift to him. I thanked the lady because I thought she wanted to leave it with him and go back home, but that was not the case. My husband asked her to come in and have a seat and have a beer with him. As I was in the process of preparing dinner for the family, the two of them talked and drank, and drank, and drank until there was no more beer. The lady walked out, and I was glad because I thought she was going home. I was grieved and disappointed a while later, when she walked back in with another six-pack of beer. After a few hours both of them were so intoxicated that the woman was unable to drive herself home, and my husband asked me to drive her home, a brief five minutes from our place down the street. When I returned home within less than ten minutes, my husband grabbed my arm, hit me and asked me where I had been so long. He was so drunk that he did not know what he was doing or why. That little occurrence proved to be a sad forecast of days and months of future miseries. That was the beginning of the turn from my excitement, my hopes and my dreams to a nightmare that was to last for years. My husband had returned home a full-blown alcoholic. What could and should have been the best day of this family's life, a dream come true, turned into a nightmare that seemed never-ending. My mood of hope at having my husband home was suddenly downgraded to a season of stress, conflict, and regret. Little did I know what was awaiting me in the months and years to come. My husband did not drink every day, but when he had a beer, he could not just have one and quit. Once he started, he did not know when to stop. His timing for drinking was unpredictable, and once he had a few drinks, he became belligerent and abusive, both verbally and emotionally and even at times physically with me as well as the children. He always said that he could quit any time he wanted to, but he simply did not want to.

My husband's drinking did not stop, and there was very little money left for the family, and all too often we lived on "C"Rations (a type of prepared canned food used by US soldiers in combat or on field exercises) because that was the most economical way to eat at that time. I had no one to turn to, I became desperate, I had no family in this country, my German friends were too far away, and I had lost all my friends in America because friends flee when alcohol enters a relationship. Alcohol mixes well with nothing but sorrow and conflict in a land where friends are few, and an unseen enemy__ addiction__ is present all the time. No one wants to be involved in such a situation and who could blame them?

Now the reader needs to keep in mind that, as all this was transpiring, I was not a Christian. I had nothing or no one to turn to for help. Such a condition complicates everything.

As a result of this dire situation, I now was forced to find work to be able to buy groceries, clothe the children and pay basic bills because my husband spent most of his paycheck on alcohol and smoking cigarettes. That also meant that I now had to put my children into Daycare, which was very painful for me. Most of the time my children cried and clung to me and did not want me to leave them at the daycare facility. I wept as I felt their pain and the thought while driving to work, came to me of what a terrible mother I had become. Every day was a painful struggle for the children and me. Hope seemed to be an illusive friend, and sadness seemed to be a constant companion!

I thought my only outlet was to share my burden with my mom. However, two problems prevented that: First, I did not have money to pay for international long distance telephone calls and, second, I really did not relish telling my Mom all that her daughter and grandchildren had to endure. As painful as it was to suffer all this alone, I found shallow comfort in keeping from my mother what would only deepen her already-complicated life. I did not want her to know and worry about my children and me. It would have grieved her. So I sat down and wrote long letters "spilling my heart out" on paper. Then, instead of mailing the letters, I tore them up because I did not want to tell her about my situation because she had ample problems of her own. My father, in schizophrenic fits of uncontrollable anger, would often threaten her with bodily harm or even death.

How could I burden my mom with my problems when she had far worse to deal with? In her desperation and at the urging of my siblings, my mama left my father for her own safety and moved away.

It was not long before I received a letter from my mother telling me that my father had died, and she requested that I not come for the funeral. She informed me that the landlord of the apartment where my father lived told my younger brother to check on his dad because they had not seen him or heard any sound from the upstairs apartment where he lived, which was very unusual. When my brother arrived at the upstairs apartment, the door was locked. Instead of breaking down the door, he called my mother who told him to call the police. When the police arrived, they broke into the apartment and found my father hanging from the window. It was assumed that he had been there for approximately a week. Therefore, my mother said there was no time for me to fly home because she had to bury him as quickly as possible.

When I received the news, I wept, I was heartbroken, not because I would miss my father, who had made it known loudly and often, that he did not love me. Receiving no love from him, I felt no love for him. Though I felt no grief that he was gone, I wept for two reasons:

First, I wept because I could feel my mother's pain. Though my mother had to leave him for her own safety and tried to get help from doctors who had diagnosed him as schizophrenic, she never expected their marriage to end this way. For the rest of her life, my mother lived in regret and guilt for leaving my father and told me she should have let him kill her. This grieved me and whenever I visited her I tried to console her, but to no avail.

Second, I wept because I now had to give up forever the hope, as slim as it was, of ever hearing my father say the words that for so long I had longed to hear, "Friede, I love you!" My anger and rejection mixed with unforgiveness toward him mounted once again. So you see, there were problems on every front with no relief in sight, and yet, there were more.

A Violent Confrontation

After my husband retired from the military, he went to technical school for retraining to be able to find employment because the civilian population did not have positions for Infantrymen or Reconnaissance Sergeants. Thankfully the Veterans' Administration provided financial assistance for that for a specified period of time. During all that time and even later during his employment in the civilian community he continued to prefer his alcohol. Most weekends he left during mid-morning and did not come home until late in the evening when he would then wake up the children and yell at them for something they had not done earlier in the week. On days when the boys played baseball or football, he used to come to the ball park to stand along the fence and watch them play and yell at them when they dropped the ball or missed it while up to bat. We were so embarrassed, and I felt so bad for my boys. Everybody attending knew that he was their father and referred to him as the 'drunkard.' My husband's usual time to be home from work during the week was around 5:30 PM so I tried to have dinner ready at that time. In the beginning, I used to wait for him to come home but after some time I decided not to wait any longer because when he arrived, he was drunk. Besides that, he knew what time dinner was to be served. Then when he decided around nine or ten o'clock to show up he wanted me to fix him dinner. I did the first two or three times but finally told him that dinner would be ready at a certain time, and if he wanted to eat with the family, he should be home. He had no reason not to be with us unless he preferred the company of his drinking companions, which he seemed to do. Years went by, and I built my life around the children. We played games in the evenings after dinner or watched some movies on television. When we heard my husband coming down the street, we rushed into our bedrooms, jumped into our beds and pretended that we were fast asleep. As he entered the house, he started yelling at the children and me and accusing us of something he remembered we had done or had not done in the past or had forgotten to do. I was such a coward and so scared that he would beat me up again that I pulled the covers over my ears to numb the noise. Even as I write this right now, I feel so ashamed about the way I acted as a mother.

Then one day I felt as if the Lord was telling me it was time to quit being a coward and time to defend my children, for better or for worse, "come hell or high water!"

Fear not, for I am with you; be not dismayed,
for I am your God. I will strengthen you, yes; I will help you,
I will uphold you with My righteous right hand.
Isaiah 41:10 NLT

It was time for this five-foot-one, ninety-pound mom to take things into her own hands. Outweighed by fifty pounds or more and knowing nothing of combat, I was seized by determination and resolve and, by golly; I was prepared to die if necessary. I did what I had to do. I was no longer gripped by fear but driven by courage. I sent my children to bed and stayed up and waited for my husband. As usual, when he came in, he started toward the boys' bedroom to drag them out of their beds. I stood in the hallway entrance with a butcher knife in my hand behind my back ready to strike him if he did not back off. When I told him to back off and leave the children alone, he said with a smirk, "And what are you going to do about it?" I dared him to try me and find out! I told him if he did not back off I would use the knife I now brandished in my right hand, the large butcher knife I had hidden behind my back and would use it with no regret. He continued to mock me and made out like he was headed for the children's room. That was not the wisest decision for him to make. Out of my mouth, in no uncertain terms, came the challenge, "over my dead body will you get to these children!" And a brief fight erupted in which I was forced to swing the knife. The sight was not pretty, and I won't bore you with details, but I can tell you one thing: From that moment on, he neither touched nor threatened to attack my children or me. Afterward, I was so surprised and thought about what had just happened. I know it was God who gave me the courage and strength because I was no longer afraid to do what I had to do in order to protect my children.

After all those years of mistreatments of the children and myself, I was at a point where I disliked my husband and wanted him out of my life and secretly hoped he would drink himself to death. I believe my children were at that point as well.

Over the years we bought a second used vehicle for me to drive to work and be able to take the children to school and places they had to go. I also had obtained a police radio, and when my husband was out at night, I listened to police radioing headquarters with vehicle license plate numbers, hoping his would not be among them. I cannot express my feelings the first time I heard them calling in his license plate number. To me, it was an indication that he was stopped by a police patrol car, most likely for drunken driving and sure enough, he did not come home that night. The next morning, he called me to come and pick him up from jail and take him to the Police Auto Impound Lot to get his car.

One year my husband decided to take the family out for the Thanksgiving meal, an offer we couldn't refuse. That was something that did not occur in our household due to the lack of finances. You can imagine that I was very happy and looked forward to it. The Wednesday evening prior to Thanksgiving my husband did not come home from work. He called me later that evening and told me that he was in the hospital with a broken leg and told me what had happened. He told me that he had gotten into a fight with another soldier. After my husband had punched him he fell to the ground and while my husband reached out his hand to help him up, that soldier kicked him in the shin and broke his leg requiring surgery to reset it. That meant now that the children and I had nothing to eat for Thanksgiving dinner, and I had no money to take the children to a restaurant. I scraped enough change together to take them to a Burger King to buy them a hamburger so that they would at least have some meat to eat on that special day. Needless to say, my husband did have his turkey dinner with all the trimmings at the hospital.

Another time my husband left the home on a Saturday morning to go to the store and get some milk. After several hours he had not returned. By the time evening rolled around, I decided to take my children for a drive, and we went looking for my husband. I figured he was at some bar, but did not know which one he frequented. So we searched all the bars for his parked vehicle. When I found it, I got out of my car with a knife in hand to slash his tires so he could not go anywhere. When I heard my children cry and beg me not to do it, I turned around and drove away without touching his vehicle.

The next morning, as I awakened, I noticed that my husband had not been at home all night. Soon the telephone rang and the person on the line said he was from Martin Army Hospital. He told me that my husband was on the second floor and that I could come to see him at any time. I could not get more information from him.

When I arrived at the hospital, I noticed that the Intensive Care Unit (ICU) was located on the second floor where I was told that he had been in surgery for eight hours during the night. The reason I had not been notified earlier was that my husband had given his parents' names as next of kin. Even then, my closest relation did not mention me as his next of kin.

I found out later that after my husband left the bar, he drove to the end of a street where he should have had made a left or right turn. Instead of turning, he went full force across the highway over an embankment into a high mound of dirt. The force of that impact bounced the truck he was driving backward against the embankment, flipped over and landed upside down in the ravine approximately 25 feet below with my husband still inside. To me, that was not an accident. He had attempted to commit suicide. My husband was very familiar with every road and turn on that installation. Night hunters on their way home noticed lights shining from the ravine and stopped to see the source of the light. When they saw my husband trying to crawl out of that ravine, they called the military police because they could not get down into the ravine to help him. When the police arrived, they had to call for a helicopter to lift him out and transport him to the hospital.

When I walked into the Intensive Care room, my husband was unconscious and hooked up to a respirator with tubes connecting to the machine. I don't recall what I expected to see, but I do remember that what I saw brought sudden shock. As I sat there looking at him, I thanked God for not allowing me to touch my husband's truck the night before because I would have felt guilty and would have assumed that it was my fault that he had that accident. I told God that I did not even know how and what to pray. I did not want to ask God to heal him because I was tired of all the abuse that my children and I had to endure, and I did not want to ask God to let him die because I thought if he died then it would be my fault as a result of my prayer. How ironic! Here I was all this time praying that God would remove the alcohol from my husband with no visible evidence that this was happening, but then I was afraid to pray believing that God might answer. How shall I explain that? So I just told God to do with him as He pleased. It pleased God to let him live.

Later I took it upon myself to look at the wreckage of that truck and noticed that the steering wheel was bent into a kidney shape as a result of the impact that caused my husband's internal bleeding, requiring immediate surgery.

After several days my husband was moved from ICU to a regular room because he was on his way to healing. On one occasion during my visits he said to me, "We have nothing going for us." I knew what he meant and was in total agreement. That remark was a signal to me that my husband was trying to end his life by making it look like an accident. I felt hurt, angry, betrayed, rejected, helpless and powerless because I was not able to do anything for him. I tried to get him to go for help about his drinking. However, he kept insisting that he did not need help and that it was my fault he was drinking. I gave up furthering my education because he told me if I would not go to night school he would quit drinking. Whatever I tried to do was a reason for him to blame me for his drinking. I am just glad he did not ask me to quit breathing. I probably would have tried to do that also in order not to give him an excuse for drinking.

A few days after my husband was moved to a regular room, he was released from the hospital. Upon his release, the surgeon told me, "There goes a miracle!"

I now had high hopes that my husband had learned a lesson and would quit drinking. But, alas, that was not to be, not just yet. Read on! I promise you it will get better!

Chapter 4

Awakening: I Need a Savior

*Come to me, all you who labor and are heavy laden,
and I will give you rest. Take My yoke upon you
and learn from Me, for I am gentle and lowly in heart,
and you will find rest for your souls.
For My yoke is easy and My burden is light.*

Matthew 11:28-30

Desperation Before Salvation

My husband had said that we had nothing going for us and I, in stubborn refusal to take divorce as the easy way out, resettled into an increasingly uncomfortable desperation. It may have been true that we had nothing going for us, but surely God and heaven had another plan. Our marriage continued to descend into deeper desperation. Hope seemed distant as neither our children nor I had much admiration for their father. We wondered how things could get any worse, but it seems that such wondering generally leads to more of the same. I found myself to be part of the problem in that I almost completely ceased to care. Hope had been crushed too many times and I lacked energy to defend my husband against the criticism of the children. We began to care little whether he came home or not. At least we did enjoy a bit of peace when he was absent.

My desperation continued. To make matters worse, a family member visiting from out of town, accused me of being the culprit in the whole sordid affair. To be honest, I wished she had been right. If it had been entirely my fault, I might have been able to do something about it. The problem was that I did not have a clue as to what to do.

While my husband was far away fighting in a war, all the responsibilities and care about the children were up to me. I breathed a sigh of relief when he came home with the thought that I could now relax and he would be the responsible one, or at least we could share the responsibility. I could not wait for him to take charge of the various situations that faced our little family, but it was not to be. My burden of caring for the family was heavier, not lighter, than it was before. He was now an alcoholic with problems, that until later, were unknown and thus undiagnosed. Later wars would give these problems a name, "PTSD" or posttraumatic stress disorder. His alcoholism was only part of the problem. Little problems, normally easily handled, became mountainous in the shadow and results of this dread disease. As an example, our oldest son caught measles and his fever was higher than the thermometer could indicate, his body temperature was way above normal and he lay there almost lifeless. I had no means to take my son to the hospital, the time was around nine PM and my husband was nowhere to be found. He was driving the only car we had at that time and I had no means to contact him. Cell phones were not available at that time and I had no idea where he was nor how to contact him. The only thing left to do was to ask my neighbor to come and stay with the other two as they were ready for bed and to call for a taxi to rush him to the hospital. This was one of the many situations that were taking place in which I could not depend on my husband for action and support. I had to act independently of him. His kin had no knowledge of my husband's behavior. Often in our most desperate circumstances, obviously beyond our abilities to resolve, remedy or revise, memories proved to be the dearest of friends. Being at my point of desperation, I remembered how my mama always tried to go to church and relied on God for strength and provision, especially when my dad had his schizophrenic attacks or was away from home without providing food for the family, or when he was at home and no one could speak or make any kind of noise lest he break into a brutal rage. I remembered how she always seemed to have a song in her heart and words of encouragement for us children. Though she spoke very little about God directly, I could tell that she had an inner strength that was unexplainable. There was something very special about her. I had almost forgotten that she had made a dual request, that first, I would remain a Catholic and, second, that I would keep my German citizenship. How could I do other than comply with my mother's request? However, my early days in America proved so busy and pressing that I had little time to think about her simple request. I had so many other things on my mind that I forgot all about my promise to my mother.

I never cease to marvel at the wisdom of God and how He brings about situations in life to constantly nudge us and bring to remembrance the request we heard and the promises we made in life. When we do recall them, we are confronted with a decision: We can either heed or ignore them. For a while I just ignored my promise until God set up situations that made me remember my departure and request from my mama. God may not have been the immediate cause of the situation in my marriage, but I believe with my whole heart the He was behind it, allowing everything that was happening to bring me to Himself. Jack, my current husband, has said many times in my hearing that everything that was happening, had happened, or would happen in our lives, within the context of our obedience, always brings us to a higher level of living.

Soon I became so desperate that I decided to go to church in hopes of finding the God that was my mama's anchor when the storms rose in her life and to have that song in my heart for my children that she always had as far back as I can remember. Perhaps just maybe I could find amid the rubble of my own desperate circumstances, the song in my heart that Mama always seemed to have in hers. So, since I was Catholic, I went to the nearest Catholic Church. What I remembered from my childhood was that immediately upon entering the church building we dipped our fingers into a small recess in the wall containing what we called "Holy Water" and then sprinkled ourselves with it in the form of a cross in honor of Jesus' death. I also remembered the fourteen stations of the cross upon the walls, statues of saints and of Mary holding baby Jesus in her arms, the raised pulpit, the confessionals and a beautiful, massive pipe organ.

To my amazement and disappointment there were no stations of the cross on the walls, no raised pulpit and no pipe organ. There was none of what I mentioned above. The instruments that were being played for worship consisted of guitars and drums that I remembered seeing only in nightclubs, never in church. No matter how hard I tried to focus on God, I simply was not able to do so and decided not to return. During the coming weeks something tugged at my heart and I had a longing to go to church and I decided to go to the church two blocks from our house, namely a Southern Baptist church. I did not know anything about any other denominational church outside the Catholic Church when I went there. To my amazement, though there were no stations of the cross, no pipe organ and no statue of Mary holding baby Jesus, God somehow opened my ears as well as my heart to hear, for the first time in my memory, that God loved me personally. I also heard that He had given His Son Jesus to die for my sins. Though I was not guilty of crimes against humanity, I had sinned against God by ignoring the love He had for me.

For the first time I realized what Jesus was all about. He had come to show us the Father and made a way for us to know Him. This was what I had always been looking for, namely love of the Father I never knew! It did not take me long to run headlong into his waiting arms. I realized then that what and Whom I was seeking had been seeking me all along. I was looking for a love I never knew and a Father I never had. Now I had both! At last I heard my new Father say, "Friede, I love you!" After more than thirty years I had found a father who loved me and had loved me all the time. It was both loud and clear and seemed for a moment to transcend all my emotions of frustration and fear. I had been loved all the time and I was just now finding out.

I noticed that people brought their own Bibles to church, a practice I had never observed before. I had never read the Bible nor was I encouraged to read it. But now I was curious as to what it said and wanted to buy one for myself. I did not realize that there were so many different versions to choose from and I asked myself: "Which is the real Bible?" Some people told me to get a King James Bible because that was the real one. Not being fluent in the English language, I had a hard time reading it with all the "thees" and "thous" and used my English-German dictionary to aid me in understanding what this strange new book was saying and how this new life worked. When I first opened my Bible I did not want to put it down because whenever I read it a tremendous peace came over me. It became my refuge in the midst of abuse, accusation and intimidation. I found renewed strength to make it through the week.

Do not sorrow, for the joy of the Lord is your strength.
Nehemiah 8:10b ESV

It was not long until my children, seeing what I had found, also surrendered their lives to Jesus Christ, and they and the church became the focus of my life.

I rarely saw my husband sober. My children, now teenagers, wanted me to get a divorce, especially Gene, the oldest one. In his mind, he was going to protect me from all the abuse of his father. This conflict was elevated to the point where he told me one day that if his father ever hit me again, he would kill him. I could not allow that to happen, and I prayed, and I prayed.

While reading the Bible, God led me to the book of 1 Corinthians, the seventh chapter in which two verses stood out to me:

And a woman who has a husband who does not believe, if
he is willing to live with her, let her not divorce him.

1 Corinthians 7:13

For how do you know, O wife,
whether you will save your husband.

1 Corinthians 7:16a

I also read the words of Jesus when He said:

And whatever things you ask in prayer,
believing, you will receive.

Matthew 21:22

After reading these verses, I felt that it was God's will for me
to stay married to my husband and not divorce him, so instead,
I began to pray for his salvation and deliverance from alcohol. I
continued to endure the abuse and prayed and waited for God
to change him and for him to stop drinking. I think I should
mention here that I did not condemn him for his condition or
taunt him with the Bible, fearing that it might trigger his pent-
up anger.

Stumbling toward Jesus

Prior to my accepting Christ, we used to take our boat to a
lake or a river every weekend and go fishing, which I still enjoy
to this day. But now I asked my husband whether he would
mind if I went to church Sunday morning and then join him
wherever and whenever he decided to go. He agreed to that.

A few months later my husband decided to come to church
with me. After a couple of weeks, he "walked the aisle" to the
front as an indication that he wanted to accept Jesus into his

heart and from that time on both of us went to church on Sunday mornings, and in the afternoon we took the boat to the lake. A few months later one of the deacons of the church invited him to accompany him for 'Monday Night Visitation' to witness to the lost and unchurched. When my husband accepted the invitation, I was so thankful and so happy. After two or three weeks when my husband returned home from one of those 'visitations', he was so intoxicated that he could barely stand up. I was crushed! The following Sunday my husband no longer desired to attend church services and said that he did not need to go to church to be with hypocrites since there were plenty of hypocrites at the bar. At least the hypocrites at the bar were honest; therefore, he chose the bar. He thought he didn't need any more hypocrites at the church and felt he could do very well on his own. I realized that my husband had taken a step toward Jesus, but he had stumbled. In a way, he was touched, but not taken over by Jesus. While I was crushed and disappointed, my prayers for his salvation continued.

Weeks, months and years went by with no change in my husband. But I did not stop praying for God to change him. His decision had not been real, but a pretense and any joy I might have had soon proved to be premature.

Then one day, God told me to shift my focus from trying to change my husband to allowing God to change me by His Holy Spirit. God clearly instructed me to seek Him more and more and keep my attention focused on Him. That relationship was more important to God than mine with my husband. I sought to try to get closer to God and walk with Him in a greater intimacy. I thought if I could focus on that He would focus more closely on my husband and work with both of us. That effectively got me out of the way so God could deal with my husband directly. I realized that he was behaving the way a lost person behaves; he didn't possess the power or the desire to do things God's way.

The Scripture says none of us do, apart from the Holy Spirit

(Romans 3:10-12; 8:7). It is only God's power working within us that enables any of us to love Him, desire Him, and want to please Him. The rest is up to the Holy Spirit working in power in his life.

Meanwhile, my children had joined a youth choir called "Sonshine" and started going on tours with the group. One of those tours took them out of town to :Vieux Carré Baptist Church" located in the heart of the French Quarter of New Orleans, Louisiana. I accompanied the choir, as I did not want the couple that led the group to have to take care of my two boys. After the services, I met the pastor, Roy Humphries, who later was the guest speaker at a Youth Retreat in Georgia.

Prior to the retreat, I asked my husband to come along as one of the chaperones. He was very indecisive. When I stopped asking him, he indicated that if I would ask him again, he would consider coming. Then, when I asked him again, he again said he would think about it. This continued for quite a while. I was at a point where I wanted to tell him that I did not care if he went to hell or not, but by the grace of God I did not say it, even though it was a very humbling experience for me. When the time for the retreat arrived, my husband did come along and met Pastor Roy Humphries, who on one beautiful afternoon asked my husband to come with him on one of the small aluminum Jon-boats for a ride on the lake. I had no idea what happened between them on the boat ride or the subject of their conversation.

A Step to Jesus

That evening during the services my husband stepped forward into the middle of the circle that consisted mostly of young people. The crowd was all young people except for a few chaperones of which he was one. We were all seated in a circle when my husband began to sob, falling to his knees and surrendering his life to Jesus Christ in front of all the young people.

I did not turn cartwheels for joy and have to admit that I was somewhat skeptical about the sincerity of his actions, remembering that it had turned out to be clearly not genuine before. However, as soon as we returned home from the retreat, my husband took every beer can and every whiskey bottle and poured out all the contents. He had made the decision to live his life for Jesus and God miraculously and suddenly took away the desire for alcohol in his life! What a miracle!

What I learned through all this was that when we switch our focus from our problems to God, though we may or may not see changes in that situation immediately, we will definitely see changes in ourselves. So my word to anyone reading this who might be in such a situation, "Never, never give up hope!"

Our marriage did not become perfect overnight. It went through a few bumps and bruises, but God smoothed them out and turned my dislike and hatred toward my husband into true love. You see, I had no problem turning my love for him into hatred, but it took God to turn my hatred for him back into love.

One More Mountain

Now I had one more mountain to climb, and that was to explain to my children that they had a "new" father and for them to work with me to involve him in family affairs. This was difficult because they struggled with having their father take a position of authority when he had not been there for them in the past. One of the greater struggles was between my husband and our oldest son. He felt he was old enough at the age of eighteen that he did not need his father now to tell him what to do. I thought the problem would take care of itself, but I was tragically wrong. The next chapter tells the sad story.

Chapter 5

A Parent's Worst Nightmare: Walking Through the Valley

Yea, though I walk through the valley
of the shadow of death ...

Psalm 23:4

A Report from the Dark Side

As I am writing this chapter, I am asking why I am telling these stories of past hurt. It certainly cannot be because they are pleasant to tell. In this process, I have been reminded that we, all of us, are gifted with our memories and are stewards of our testimonies. I open here one of the most difficult chapters of my life, spanning seven decades. It has been painful recounting, but I am learning to "count it all joy" to consider that all things work together for good and especially the experiences that are exceedingly painful. Malcolm Muggeridge reflected that most of the things of value that he had learned in all his life were the results of his deepest pains. These and other issues have encouraged me to revisit this painful era of my past and draw from the account to hopefully be of value to those walking through similar circumstances. Or better still, I am pleased with the possibility that this story could sound warnings that might prevent such a cruel intrusion of tragedy that my family endured. No problem that exists should be treated lightly. I live with the fact that we might have avoided this tragedy had someone told me what I am telling you.

Throughout the years I made it a point to get the children to share what was on each of their hearts, the good, the bad and the ugly. I liked to take each of them on a date, to the movies and then for a soda or whatever they preferred. When it was my oldest son Gene's day, I felt he was holding back, and I could never get him to share how he really felt. I knew something was bothering him, but I could never get him to open up and share his feelings.

Allow me to go back in years to when he was about five months old. I had a dream during one night in which my husband and I were walking with Gene in the forest when all of a sudden he snatched his hand out of mine and started to run ahead. Not being familiar with the area, I called him back and ran after him. As soon as I had caught up with him, I grabbed his hand and instructed him to stay beside us. He did so until my husband and I entered into a focused discussion. In the midst of the dream, I realized that Gene was no longer with us. I called out for him but did not get an answer until I heard him screaming and calling for help. I started running in the direction where the voice came from and saw Gene in the middle of an area filled with quicksand. I tried to reach him by stretching out my hand but was unable to do so because of the distance. I frantically looked for a tree limb or any stick to hold out for him to grab hold of. By the time I had found one, Gene had slipped further away and was not able to reach it. I looked for a longer object. When I found one, I still could not reach him. I had to watch my son disappear, helplessly standing there unable to save him.

That dream was so strong, and it seemed so real. I immediately jumped up to check on him and found him sound asleep in his crib. Soon after that I did not pay any more attention to that dream and said to myself that it was just a dream.

Now when he was eighteen years of age, he always said he couldn't wait until he was nineteen years old because that was the "legal" age back then. I didn't know all that he was thinking, but I thought he was looking forward to being on his own and doing what he really wanted to do without restraints.

I could sense that he had an inner conflict and tried continuously to encourage him to show respect, not just for his father, but for himself as well as for me. I did not realize how severe the pain was within him. Whenever I asked him "What's wrong" he would invariably respond, "Nothing."

Then one night our youngest son knocked on our bedroom door after midnight yelling that his brother was bleeding and had cut his wrist. I remember that night like it was yesterday. It was around two o'clock in the morning, and he was bleeding profusely. I tried to stop the bleeding as best I could and rushed him to the hospital where he was treated and dismissed. From that point on I lived my life as if I were walking on thin ice, not knowing when it would happen again.

Because of our son's attempted suicide, we had to go to counseling as a family. Having never been in such a situation before and not knowing any good counselors, we went to one that was recommended to us as a good Christian Counselor. When the counselor inquired about our family life, we informed him that though our son was nineteen years of age, we expected him to abide by our rules, such as attending school daily unless there was a legitimate reason for his absence, showing respect to his parents, participating in family affairs and letting us know when and where he was going. In other words, we were asking him simply to join us doing life together with us as a family. As long as he lived under our roof, we expected him, as well as his brother and sister, to abide by our rules. In the presence of our son, the counselor recommended that we relax some of our rules with our oldest son, basically letting him have his way, considering he was an "adult." The counselor also told us in the presence of our son that unless we did that, he would either take his own life or kill someone else. I was furious! That man just gave our son a license to hold us hostage and from that moment on our son continuously used the threat of suicide as a form of manipulation. I did not have access to the spiritual tools that are available today. Ours was a generation of rules and regulations, especially with the influence of the military in our lives. We just could not abide rule breaking! Little did I know that the ship of this family was about to run aground. Oh that I could have known beforehand!

One day we received a telephone call from the school that he was found drinking beer in the locker room and as a result was suspended from school for three days. Some time later I received a call from a Pawn Shop owner asking me whether I was missing an expensive gold bracelet to which I answered, "No." He told me that he had an identification card (ID) belonging to a Gene McDonald, and he asked me whether or not that was my son. When I asked my son where his ID card was, he told me at first that he had lost it. I reminded him that it was his responsibility to immediately report the loss of it, or I was going to do it. At that point, he told me that he had loaned his ID card to one of his friends who was under age and wanted to enter a bar with his older brother. However, instead of entering the bar, this so called friend was actually involved in a break-in at a home, steeling valuable items. He then used my son's ID card as identification to pawn off the items for cash, in this case, expensive jewelry. That's why the pawnshop owner telephoned me for verification. The next day a police detective came to our house to talk to my husband about this break-in. That particular detective knew my husband and told him that he would trust him to bring our son to the police station, or he would go to the school and pick him up from there. We appreciated his gesture and told him we would bring him to the station. At first, my son decided not to cooperate with the detective. Even after he was told that unless he cooperated and released the name of his so-called friend, he would be the one being convicted and going to jail. Our son still refused to squeal on his friend. Our son was willing to go to jail instead. After trying to explain to him the seriousness of this situation, he was still afraid to give the name because that boy's brother was part of a dangerous gang and they would come after him and kill him. Therefore, he was willing to go to jail and said if they put him in jail he would just kill himself. The detective, however, was a very compassionate person and helped us to finally bring our son to his senses and reveal the name of the young man that had his ID card and worked with the detective. I felt somewhat relieved and hoped that we could close that chapter in our life with our son. But it was not to be.

Sometime later we received another call from the police informing us that they had traced our son, the same one I might add, to a theft of a store. As every mother would do, I wanted to take sides for my son but could not do so based on his previous conduct. I never was one to say, "My boy does not do that!" I had learned my lesson, and I strongly believe that no parent can say with 100% assurance that their children would not do this or that. It never occurred to me to think that our son would break into a store and remove items. I thought that this only happens to other families, not ours! Making a long story short, our son was sentenced to go to a juvenile detention center for one month. This was one of the most painful and difficult things for me to do up to this point in my life, to bring my son there, register him, leave him there and walk away! But what else could I do? I cannot express in words how deeply I was hurting. I wept all the way home, asking myself, "Where did I go wrong?" The other two children turned out to honor and respect what we had taught them. It could not have been his upbringing in our home that made him do that. I was perplexed and without answers.

All these troubles occurred during my son's senior year of High School and now he was not allowed to graduate on time but had to repeat his senior year because he had missed too many days. I now had three seniors in High School scheduled to graduate at the same time because Gene had to repeat his senior year, Sheila, our daughter, was on time and Steve, our youngest son, was advanced from second to fourth grade and from that year on attended classes with our daughter who remained on schedule.

As is customary, I began preparation with my children for their graduation by ordering three class rings, selecting senior photos, ordering graduation announcements, caps and gowns, thank-you cards, senior yearbook, and whatever else had to be arranged. Though Gene gave me many headaches, it was an exciting time for me to have three children as seniors to graduate at the same time.

The Plot Thickens

After my son Gene's nineteenth birthday, he mentioned on one Saturday that he wanted to go to a party with a friend. I knew that young man from church and therefore asked my son to please refrain from drinking alcoholic beverages. His response was "O mom!" I left it at that, and I did not give him a specific time to be at home as he now was considered an adult.

The next morning, as my husband and I got ready to go to church, I did not awaken my son. I just thought I would let him sleep. When we returned from church, he was still in his pajamas and just moping around. I told him then to get cleaned up and become somewhat presentable. He started talking back to me, using hateful, ugly words. Having never done this before, he succeeded in inciting my anger. I was shocked and told him he would not talk to me like that and popped him on his cheek. He stormed into his room and after a while came out and went outside. I assumed he went outside to the garage where he had his weight bench to lift weights and blow off steam. After a short time, he came back into the house, went into his room, came back and went outside again.

The Worst Moment of my Life

I have no recollection of time. His best friend came to visit and I told him that Gene was in the garage. In less than five minutes the young man knocked on the door again and asked for my husband. I wanted to know whether anything was wrong and he just said he needed to talk with my husband who walked outside with him. Within a few minutes, my husband came back into the house, went to the telephone and called for an ambulance. Now I suspicioned that something was very wrong and assumed that the weights he was trying to lift were too heavy for him to control and caved in and crushed his chest. My husband told me not to go outside! That was the wrong thing to tell me. Nothing could keep me from getting to my son, especially when I now knew that something was seriously wrong! I found my son lying unconscious on the concrete floor, a rope dangling from the garage rafter and his best friend beside him. I remember the purple furrow around his neck from the rope marks and see them still. I could not believe my eyes. It could not be true. Here I stood next to my lifeless son lying on that concrete floor with his best friend standing beside him, both of us speechless. I felt pain for this young man who had found my son hanging at the end of the rope and called for my husband to come and help him to cut him down.

When the ambulance arrived, our son had no heartbeat and the emergency personnel used the paddles to shock him and got a pulse. As I stood there watching them, my own heart almost stopped beating, the air seeming to leave my lungs. I could not believe this was happening! They put him in the ambulance and drove off with sirens blaring. By this time, it seemed that the whole neighborhood had gathered at our house trying to find out what was happening. I was numb! My best friend, Charlotte, who lived three houses down the street from ours, came to see what the problem was and mentioned that I should probably go to the hospital to check on my son. As I tried to get the keys to my car, she would not allow me to drive. Instead, she drove me to the hospital. But I told her that first I wanted to go to my son's best friend's home to check on him. I wanted to talk with his mother to let her know what her son had just experienced and wanted to pray with them. At this moment I was grieving more for this young man than for myself. What a shock it must have been for him to find his best friend in that condition! I cannot even imagine! Charlotte drove me to the hospital and stayed with me until I was ready to go home. My husband did not come with us but stayed at home.

After a few hours, the doctor came and told me that my son's brain was swollen due to a loss of oxygen. He wanted to know approximately how long my son was without oxygen, a question for which I had no answer. He told me that it usually would take about seventy-two hours for the swelling to go down and that it could go either way. The swelling might go down, or he may not recover. He then allowed me to go into the Intensive Care room where my son was connected to life support, oxygen and I.V. A nurse then asked me whether I wanted to allow visitors to his room or not. I told her that I did not want anyone to see my son in this comatose state. While at the hospital, police officers came to inquire about the circumstances of my son's situation and documented everything I had told them.

My prayer now was for God to reduce the swelling in my son's brain and to heal him totally. Then during the night, I begged God not to take my son from me and, no matter what, I just did not want to lose him! I was willing to feed him, dress him and do whatever was necessary as long as I could just have him near me.

When I arrived at the hospital the next day to visit my son, there were two teenage girls standing by his bed, one on each side, talking and giggling. I was furious and asked them to leave and went looking for the nurse in charge. I was so hurt that anyone would be so negligent to our family's wishes and was ready for heads to roll. I then found out that one of the girls had a sister who was a nurse at that hospital and allowed them to come through a back door!

After I came home, I tried to get my mind off this incident and again asked God not to take my son from me, I cried, "after all he was my first boy," as if God did not know that. There seemed to be no improvement, and I felt as if I was drowning in my sorrow and pain. It seemed like my tears would never end, and I looked to God for help. Then I came across this Psalm that was written by King David:

> *Save me, O God! For the waters have come up to my neck,*
> *I sink in the deep mire, where there is no foothold;*
> *I have come into deep waters, and the flood sweeps over me.*
> *I am weary with my crying; my throat is parched.*
> *My eyes grow dim with waiting for my God.*
>
> Psalm 69:1-3 NRSV

I thought after all David had gone through, he continued to trust God even when all hope seemed lost. This gave me new courage not to give up hope.

After struggling, wrestling, and pleading with God day and night for three full days, I discovered that one of Gene's teacher's had left a note for me at the hospital on Wednesday of that week. In that note she wrote some wonderful words about my son and shared Isaiah 55:8-9.

Comfort and Sorrow

Once home, I opened my Bible to these verses before going to sleep. This is what I read:

"For my thoughts are not your thoughts,
Nor are your ways My ways." Says the Lord
"For as the heavens are higher than the earth,
So are my ways higher than your ways,
And My thoughts than your thoughts."

Then God and I had a conversation. He listened as I yelled at Him in my desperation! I listened as He spoke to me. He asked me if I was prepared to allow him to walk with me and work through my pain and still be God? After a long struggle, I gave up because I realized that God knew what lay ahead and what was best for all of us. I knew that this son was not just mine, but was a gift from God all along. That night, in my helpless situation, I was ready to do as He desired and surrendered my son and myself totally and completely into His hands. I told Him that I trusted Him to do what He thought was best and if it were His pleasure to leave my son with me or take him I would submit to His will. After all, He knows the end from the beginning and knows what is best, and no matter what He decided to do, He would give me the strength to go on living.

The moment I said "Lord, he is yours" and surrendered my son into the care of the Lord, I had such a peace come over me that, to this day, is beyond explanation. I looked at the clock, and it was 2:00 AM. I fell asleep and ever since that night I have never had a sleepless night. It seems that God has granted to me the gift of anointed sleep. What an awesome God He is to give me such amazing grace to allow me to freely release my Son into His care.

I truly believe that there is no help for the unbearable pain a parent experiences after the suicide of a child outside Jesus Christ.

He heals the brokenhearted and binds up their wounds.
Psalm 147:3 NIV

My husband called me during the day on Thursday, the next day, as I had to go to work, and told me that our pastor was coming to visit in the evening and for me not to cook dinner. He would just pick up something on the way home. Needless to say, anytime I could get out of cooking dinner I welcomed that, and I still do. During our conversation with the pastor, the question came up about whether I wanted to donate our son's organs. This came as a shock to me, and I told them that I still was expecting my son to live, and I had not even thought about donating any organs and needed more time to process the thought. It was then that my husband told me that there was simply no more time. He also told me that he had gone to the hospital to visit our son, and the doctors had informed him that they did an electroencephalogram (EEG), a test used to detect abnormalities related to electrical activity of the brain, and this test revealed no activity whatsoever. Then the doctor told him that Georgia State law required a second test after twenty-four hours. If the second test were identical to the first test with no activity present, they would then declare my son dead.

I experienced a moment of anger at my son for taking his own life when I knew another young man who was sentenced to a life in a wheelchair as a result of a car accident due to no fault of his own, struggling to live. He, like my son, enjoyed sports and was very handsome. I thought about the audacity of my healthy, handsome son to leave us without saying a word, and why not give someone else who wants to live the chance to do so? Therefore, I consented to donate my son's organs so that others might live. I knew my son would have agreed.

We had to be at the hospital early the next morning to be present for the results of the EEG. If this second test detected no brain activity, they would have to continue to keep him on a breathing machine to keep oxygen going to the organs until they removed his organs to be recovered for transplants. We were told that brain death is irreversible and is legally and medically recognized as death. The machine merely keeps the organs viable until they can be harvested.

When we arrived the next morning, we were received at the hospital with a red carpet welcome but had to wait for the completion of the second EEG. As I sat in that private room I was completely numb and told the Lord again, "Whatever You have willed, just give me strength; I cannot go through this without You." When the doctor came into the room, he informed us that there was no brain activity whatsoever and that they had pronounced him dead. He asked us if we wanted to go in to see our son for one last time. That was the hardest thing I have ever done in my life!

As I am writing this now and recalling those moments, I am experiencing the waves of sorrow all over again. I can see the room, my boy's body; feel the pain, the heartbreak, and the grief. I can still see the heart pumping, yet knowing he was no longer really alive, and I would never be able to see him or speak with him again. I felt so helpless! I had hoped, but now all hope was gone! My last words were simply, "I love you!"

I guess there are some things we just will never get over. I am wondering now if we ever should. But praise the Lord we don't have to live and linger in that moment for the rest of our lives or wait to experience the Psalmist's words:

Weeping may endure for a night,
but joy comes in the morning.

Psalm 30:5b

Now, amid these sad memories, I am standing in that promised morning, and that joy, as I complete this chapter. I will ever live in that joy that comes from my God. It is His joy in me that continues to give me strength to go on!

For the joy of the Lord is your strength!

Nehemiah 8:10b

Looking back, I am soaking in thanksgiving that I was so fortunate to have had those few precious days to prepare for the inevitable. Many others have been denied such times by the suddenness of death without any prior warning. After the memorial, I gathered all my son's laundry to wash. When I hung his football jersey outside on the clothesline to dry, I started crying again, remembering and reminiscing about watching him play. When I went back inside, I made myself a cup of coffee and sat down and thought about all the wonderful moments we had together and, at the same time, wept bitterly about the thought of not ever being able to see him again. Then it seemed as if God's presence was so strong and He was right there with me telling me "I am here with you, and I have carried you on my shoulders through these past few days, now I am putting you on your own two feet again. But don't be afraid, I will walk with you. I will give you my strength and will help you as you go on. Just continue to hold on to me!" I remember responding by saying "No, not yet, I am not ready!" Then I remembered the poem "Footprints in the Sand" by Carolyn Carty.

One night a man had a dream. He dreamed He was walking along the beach with the LORD. Across the sky flashed scenes from His life. For each scene, He noticed two sets of footprints in the sand, one belonging to Him and the other to the LORD.

When the last scene of His life flashed before Him, he looked back at the footprints in the sand. He noticed that many times along the path of His life there was only one set of footprints. He also noticed that it happened at the very lowest and saddest times of His life.

This really bothered Him, and He questioned the LORD about it, "LORD you said that once I decided to follow you, you'd walk with me all the way. But I have noticed that during the most troublesome times in my life there is only one set of footprints. I don't understand why, when I needed you most, you would leave me."

The LORD replied, "my precious, precious child, I Love you, and I would never leave you! During your times of trial and suffering when you see only one set of footprints, it was then that I carried you."

A Comforting Afterthought

I was raised to believe that suicide was sin and during the following days and weeks I was plagued with wanting to know where my son was spending eternity. Suicide is bad enough, but when it is shrouded in total mystery, more pain is added.

Then the Lord led me to these verses:

For the Lord does not see as man sees; for man looks at the outward appearance, but the Lord looks at the heart.
1 Samuel 16:7b

Shall not the Judge of all the earth do right?
Genesis 18:25

These verses helped me to re-direct my focus and try to move on with my life. Overwhelming emotions still left me reeling for several months. No matter how hard I tried, my grief was heart wrenching as well as mind numbing. I kept thinking and wondering that if I had not reacted to my son's outburst as I did, would this have happened? Was it my fault that my son died? I was on an emotional roller coaster. My emotions went from shock to anger, to guilt, to confusion, to feelings of rejection. It seemed that wherever I went people were whispering while looking toward me discussing that, "there is the mother whose son committed suicide." I felt alone even among most of my friends and church family. And frankly, there is nothing anybody could do or say to make me feel better. Because I did not find comfort from man, I dove into God's Word to receive comfort and found it in the following verses:

Therefore, now you have sorrow,
but I will see you again,
and your heart will rejoice,
and your joy no one will take from you.

John 16:22b

For I will turn their mourning to joy, will comfort them,
and make them rejoice rather than sorrow.

Jeremiah 31:13b

I personalized these words from Jeremiah and took them as a promise from God to me, saying:
You will turn my mourning into joy. You will comfort me
and exchange my sorrow for rejoicing.

It still took me several months, but the joy of the LORD actually did become my strength (Nehemiah 8:10). Without it, I would have floundered!

My concern now was for my other children and my husband. I was watching them very closely. My fear was that my husband might start drinking again to numb the pain of losing his son. But by the grace of God that was not the case. As a matter of fact, our relationship continued to improve, and we began to learn to be intimate with God together, often stopping whatever we were doing to hold hands, weep and pray together. What a blessing in the midst of a tragedy that only God could provide!

My younger son, Steve, and daughter, Sheila struggled greatly. Gene was Sheila's best friend, and she considered him her protector during their teen years. She had a hard time coping but realized that life had to be lived with a determination to make the best of each day. Steve, on the other hand, was angry at his brother's action as he saw the devastating effect it had on all of us and for the longest time did not want to talk about it.

I requested of both of them their current response to this tragedy in our family that took place so many years ago. Before I present their response, it seems fitting to tell you that it has been thirty-three years since the life of their brother, my son, was taken from us. Their responses were so appropriate, helpful and touching that I felt you should read them.

Here is Gene's only sister's response, Sheila as she recalled the crisis in our family's life:

> Looking back at my childhood, I can remember having absolutely no worries ... well, maybe a few little worries that were really insignificant at the time like getting braces, what hairstyle to wear, doing well in school, etc. I remember riding my bike around the neighborhood and annoying my brothers because I always wanted to include myself in their activities. Our high school years were the best. My older brother Gene had to repeat his senior year in high school as a result of some difficulties that caused him to miss too many days to graduate on time. I, being the middle child, remained where I was. My younger brother, Steve, was ahead of his peers in elementary school so the teachers suggested he skip from second to fourth grade so that he could be more challenged. As a result of his advancement, he and I attended the rest of our school years in the same grade. This caused the three of us to attend the senior year of high school at the same time and resulted in us having a lot of the same friends. Gene was the most charismatic. He had lots of friends. The girls loved him. He was popular and always seemed to have something on his "social" calendar.
>
> I was shocked when he committed suicide. I knew he had made an attempt before, but I didn't really think it was an attempt because

he had everything going for him. Looking back, I now realize it was a cry for help. I still don't understand it. I thought he just got mad and wanted to get attention. I didn't think he really wanted or would, for that matter, hurt himself. I remember waking up in the night and hearing a commotion in the bathroom only to find my mom standing over my brother and blood was, what seemed like, everywhere. My mom was holding towels on his wrists. It still is a blur. Gene went to the hospital and then went to an inpatient treatment program. When he returned home, he seemed like the "normal" fun, outgoing Gene. Then... it happened during our senior year in high school. The unthinkable. He was gone. It's odd what you remember. Gene had a black 'Member's-Only' leather jacket. I loved that jacket. It was so cool! I asked Gene if I could wear it and it was always a "no." Then, one day I was going out with my friends and Gene was going out with his friends, and he said I could wear it. Oh my God! We all ran into each other at a local place that allowed "underage" kids to get in even though they served alcohol. I remember having on the coveted jacket and running into my brother and even remember a group of us, including Gene, dancing. It was the best time ever. I didn't know then that it would be the last time I saw my brother laughing and carefree.

I was at work when I heard the news. I worked part-time at the local Burger King. A youth leader and friend of ours who always came over and hung out with us came to my work and said: "I have something to tell you when you get off work." I had about an hour left of my shift. I got my discounted meal and sat down to eat when he told me that Gene had hanged himself and was in the hospital. I remember being so confused... Why did this person wait over an hour to tell me? Why did he let me sit down to eat when my brother was dead or dying in the hospital?! Was Gene going to be OK? What happened? I immediately jumped up and drove to the hospital as fast as I could. It's all so foggy to me. I remember getting bits and pieces of information. Argument. His friend came over and went around the back of the house to the garage and found Gene ...

hanging. My friend got my dad who had to cut him down. Hospital. Life Support. No brain function. Coma. Death.

To this day, I can't think about it or talk about it without getting emotional. Every time I see a movie or anything that unexpectedly shows someone hanging or about to be hanged I am overwhelmed with sadness and regret and think about Gene. It brings me back to the cruelty of some of the kids in high school. How I would walk by his locker in the hall at school after his funeral and see where some of the kids started a "hangman" game on the locker and the stares and whispers. I think about what my dad must have felt seeing his son like that and having to cut him down. I think about his friend finding him and what a traumatic event that must have been and continues to be for him. I think of my mom. Her son ... gone. No goodbyes. No final "I love you." No explanations. No hugs, just pain, and misery. How does one overcome that? As a mother of three, I can't even imagine how I could survive the loss of one of my children. I often drift away and wonder what made him do it. What was so bad or wrong in his life that caused him to end it? No matter what it was, everything can get better. He had a family that loved him. He had friends. He had a personality that was larger than life and a smile that could light up a room. He was good looking. He was smart. What went wrong? I've since learned that you never know what's going on behind someone's smile. You never know what inner demons are at work. You can be what appears to be fun loving and happy outwardly but harbor such secrets and pain inside. I've learned not to judge but to show compassion to everyone. We all have struggles. We all have doubts. Some people decide to end the struggles and doubts. I just want answers. Answers I know I'll never get. I just wish he had let the thought pass and made it just one more day because I know that day would've been better, and he would still be here ... or would he? Would his troubles and pain have haunted him? If not that day, would it have been three weeks later, a year later? I wish he had shared with me what was wrong. I wish he had told me what he was thinking of doing. I would have talked him out of it. I felt an emptiness in my life. There's a spot that was reserved for my brother, Gene, but he is not here. I will always wonder why ... I will always say, "I love you" to those close to me because I know we are not guaranteed a tomorrow or a tomorrow with the same people in our lives. I will always see that smile of his, but I can't help but also know that it was just a mask hiding darkness and pain that was within. I will always miss him.

Sheila (Gene's little sister)

Now here is his only brother's (Steve) response:

Some things you can't forget. Some things you can't understand.

I remember it like it was yesterday. It was a Sunday, and I was scheduled to work at the store by myself that day. Sunday's are normally slow days, and we were only open for 8 hours. This day was no different as I started the workday. I opened the store and just waited for customers. It was a slow day, just like every other Sunday. But then I received a phone call from my mother to tell me that my older brother tried to kill himself. He had gone out to the garage and hung himself. One of our friends had come over to visit, and my mom told him that Gene was in the garage. Our friend was the first person to find him. Our friend ran back to the house and got my dad, and they both lowered my brother. You would have to know some of our family history to understand what happened next. I did not call my boss to ask for time off to go to the hospital or to rush home. I don't remember calling my boss at all to let her know what happened. I just stayed at work and watched the time go by until I closed the store. Because it was a slow day like every Sunday, it was just my thoughts and me.

I first thought back to a few years before when my brother woke me up in the middle of the night and calmly told me that he needed help because he had cut his wrist. I remembered being annoyed with him because he interrupted my sleep. I marched across the hallway, woke up my parents and just as calmly told them that Gene had cut his wrist. That was a rough time for our family. Things eventually got better, and we started attending a local church. My brother's life seemed to change for the better.

No customers in the store so I still had plenty of time to think about how my brother went from those days to the decision to end his own life on this Sunday. I remembered that over the past year, my brother's behavior started to change. He was hanging around with some people who weren't the best influence. He was staying out later than he was supposed to and doing some things that he should not have done and that led to fighting with my parents. We weren't as close as we used to be and we fought also. I remembered that just a few weeks before we had a serious fight that included wrestling, punching, and a black eye.

As I look back, I know that I was very angry. I thought this was such a selfish act. I knew that it would affect my parents, especially when I found out that my mother had a conflict with my brother that morning. There was no way to understand what she was feeling. There was no way to imagine how our friend was affected. I cannot fathom having that image in your mind. There was also no way to understand how this would affect my life. I wasn't even thinking about that. I just could not comprehend how a young man with so much promise could do something like that.

I think God has given me the ability to accept things that happen in my life. I firmly believe that things happen for a reason. Sometimes things happen due to God's providence and grace. And sometimes things happen because of our selfish humanity and mistakes. Though there are things in the past that I will never understand, I have always trusted that the future holds promise. I just wish my brother would have believed that.

Steve (Gene's younger brother)

If you or anyone with whom you are acquainted are

experiencing suicidal thoughts, please stop long enough to read this letter below that Steve, my youngest, and now the only son, wrote, trying to put himself into his brother's shoes several years after he voluntarily took his own life. He imagined what his brother might have to say if he was to write his younger brother.

A Letter from Beyond

Dear Steve,

Hey, how have you been? It has been a while. I wanted to just take a moment to tell you that I am sorry. I know that, by now, you have probably moved on with life and I may be nothing more than a passing thought or an occasional mention in a conversation. But I can't help but wonder what our lives would have been like if I didn't make that decision. What would I be doing? I wonder what kind of job I would have? Would I have a family like yours with an amazing wife and wonderful children? What would my children be doing? I can almost imagine having a little girl and seeing her grow up into a beautiful young lady. Or maybe a son who grew up to be a baseball player and we could have spent time playing catch. You do remember that I liked playing baseball, don't you? You probably also remember we played football when we were younger. Oh, the days when we were young, and our major concerns were fighting fights we could win and getting the cutest girlfriend. Sorry, I am getting away from the reason I wanted to write. It's just so easy to wonder what my life would have been. But, of course, all I can do is wonder.

I know that what I did doesn't make a lot of sense. I was just dealing with some things that would have been hard to explain. I know I made some bad choices and that kind of caught up with me. It's hard to believe I could make that big of a mess of my life in only 18 years. I know we all had our problems growing up. Dad was hard on us. But you know as well as I do that he had a rough life. Maybe if his life was different, mine would have turned out different as well. Sorry, there I go wondering again. I know I can't blame my choice on him.

As I was saying, I was going through a tough time. I didn't think I could talk to you. You seemed to have a better handle on things, and I am not sure you would have understood what I was facing. And we had just had that fight a couple of weeks before. Why did we fight so much? It seems like there was way too much fighting going on in our house. We were some stubborn kids. Remember that time we got in a fight because you wanted to change the TV channel? Doesn't seem so important now, does it? Maybe if we didn't fight so much, we would have talked more. Wow, I did it again. Our fighting didn't force me into my decision ... it was my decision alone. I will try to stay on track here.

My point is that I am extremely sorry for what I did. It was selfish. I wasn't thinking about dad, mom, Sheila or you. I was just thinking about me, and I didn't want to deal with stuff anymore. I know that my decision had a huge impact on your life ... on all of your lives. Your life is different because of what I did. I know mom doesn't understand why I did it. I can only imagine how much it hurt her. Especially knowing the situation with her own dad. I robbed all of you. I robbed mom and dad of a son. I robbed you and Sheila of a big brother. I robbed your children of an uncle. I probably would have been a good uncle. Oh man, I almost forgot about Jimmy. You remember he was the one that found me. I don't even want to think about the impact of that initial sight on his life. That wasn't fair. I should not have done that.

I wish I could go back in time, but that's not possible. I wish I would have realized that those things I was dealing with weren't going to last forever. So many people go through so much worse and make it. I wish I had looked beyond that Sunday morning. I wish I had realized that I had a life ahead of me. I wish I would have thought about my future wife and kids ... and baseball games ... and dance recitals ... and nephews and nieces ... and family vacations ... and a family dog. I am pretty sure I would have owned a beagle. Do you remember the beagle?

If I could ask one thing of you, it would be to please share my story with others. Please tell them that problems are temporary. Please tell them there is a future regardless of what life looks like at that point in time. Please tell them that there are people who need them ... people who love them ... people who care about them. Please tell them to look past their own Sunday morning. Please tell them it will get better. Please tell them there is hope.

Steve, please forgive me. I was wrong. Please tell mom and Sheila that I am sorry also. I miss you more than you know.

Love,

Gene

Perhaps reading this wonderful imaginary response from beyond the veil is encouraging you as it encouraged me and continues to do so.

When it came time for the graduation exercises from High School, my joy was dampened by the thought that Gene was supposed to be in attendance to receive his diploma. I rejoiced for Sheila and Steve, but in the back rooms of my mind, I was grieving the fact that Gene was not there. It was a bittersweet time for all of us.

Later on, I thought about Gene's date of birth and date of death and realized how short life really is. You see, his numbers read: Born 01-02 (January second), Died: 03-04 (March fourth). In other words, 1,2,3,4 and he was gone. Therefore, let us live our life with meaning and make a difference for those around us, not for our satisfaction, but for the glory of God.

Now you have read the story, painful in the telling but freighted with expectations that it may be helpful in ministering to those of you who still go through the torment of unanswered questions, unresolved guilt or are held prisoners in the grip of disappointment.

It is said that time is a healer. While that is true, it is also a revealer. Nothing opens us to an understanding of ourselves like a stark tragedy. Time spent in the grace of grieving is not a waste of time, especially if we grieve toward God and open the deep places of our souls to Him. After all, He was and is a Father Who, with loving determination to redeem a lost world, orchestrated the death of His Own Son on a Roman cross, solely for you and me. We must never forget, amid empathy for Jesus in His unimaginable pain, physically and emotionally, the indescribable pathos in his mother's heart as she watched Him die and the deep, crushing disappointment of his followers, the deepest hurt in God the Father's heart, a hurt the human heart can never fathom. It is none other than the Father's Spirit Who speaks to the grieving heart, "Child, I know how you feel, and it's all going to be all right." And He could also say, "And, by the way, I will see to it that you are comforted with my comfort, and you will understand it better bye and bye."

Blessed be the God and Father of our Lord Jesus Christ,
the Father of mercies and God of all comfort,
who comforts us in all our affliction,
so that we may be able to comfort
those who are in any affliction,
with the comfort with which
we ourselves are comforted by God.
2 Corinthians 1:3-4 ESV

As we leave this sad episode, allow me to speak of suicide in general, a specter that is ever with us and around us. Pay attention to the sad statistics:

- Suicide is the tenth leading cause of death in all age-levels.

- It is the second leading cause of death in ages 17-24.
- There is a suicide in America every thirteen minutes.

All of you who are reading this know someone who has been affected by suicide in the family.

Many of you are in a family touched by this mysterious intruder who leaves more questions that can never be answered here and invites hundreds of questions later.

Some of you have had a husband, wife, son, daughter, father or mother who have taken this tragic route simply because staying on the earth was too threatening an existence. You are not over it and should never expect to get over it. Expecting to get over it will only lead to more disappointments with all its sad friends visiting you frequently. While you cannot get over it, you can—and I say it emphatically-—get through it! While you must never allow yourself to be defined by this event, you must remember never to deny it as a significant experience with which you have reconciled and from which you have learned more about yourself and life in general than perhaps anything else in your past. You will choose to be better because of it and not *bitter*. You will give up pity for *empowerment* to help others in their darkest moments. You have been forcefully added to a long list of students in the university of suffering and will be awarded a degree of passionate empathy and deep understanding that cannot be attained by anything but experience. You will accept the event and the process of valuing it as a gift wrapped in sadness. When unwrapped, it begins to yield untold treasures, which will be obvious not only to you but to the world that is watching how you, as a believer in a Sovereign God, process this whole event. You will win the right to make the most comforting statement a grieving heart needs to hear, "I may not know exactly how you feel, nor does anybody except God, but I have been there, and I understand!"

Now, that you are a steward of your story, allow God to use it to encourage and empower others and establish you among the encouragers of the world.

You have turned for me my mourning into dancing;
you have put off my sackcloth and clothed me with gladness.
Psalm 30:11

A Response from Jack:

I have read this chapter through tears, sometimes losing composure altogether, unable to go on. I have concluded that it is the most touching and moving chapter I have ever read in any book! I have asked Burkhart Publishers and my son, the Editor, and CEO, to allow us to turn this chapter into a booklet for those who have experienced this dark intruder's unwelcomed visit. I do that knowing that it will comfort thousands if not millions of folks who are still wincing from the memories of a loved one who chose this unfortunate departure and if reading it causes one person, just one, to resist the temptation to take this dark path and choose life, it will be worth it all.

My pride in Friede, my wife and Gene's mother, Sheila, Gene's younger sister, and Steve, Gene's younger brother, is indescribable. Thanks for walking us through your tragedy with heads held high and hearts filled with compassion and hope.

Jack Taylor
Husband of Friede and Papa to Sheila and Steve

Lift up your heads, O you gates!
And be lifted up, you everlasting doors!
And the King of glory will come in.
Who is this King of glory?

The Lord, strong and mighty,
The Lord, mighty in battle.
Lift up your heads, O you gates!
And lift them up you everlasting doors!
And the King of glory shall come in.
Who is his King of glory?
The Lord of hosts,
HE IS THE KING OF GLORY.

Psalm 24:7-10

Chapter 6

Getting Over, Down Again, and Going On

... Forgetting the past and looking forward to what lies
ahead, I press on to reach the end of the race
and receive the heavenly prize for which God,
through Christ Jesus, is calling us.

Philippians 3:13-14 NLT

The months following the life-shattering experience of my son's suicide were filled with a whole array of emotions ranging from anger and sadness, through to guilt and finally, acceptance. None of that happened overnight. My healing process was slow, deliberate, painful and purposeful. My doctor wanted to put me on the prescription drug "Valium" to help me cope with this tragedy, but I refused to numb my mind and decided to work through the grief.

I now had to refocus on High School graduation preparation for Sheila and Steve. It was very painful for me to have to cancel the order for Gene's ring, cap and gown and graduation announcements. It seemed as if I lived with constant reminders of that event back in March. There were dozens of details that required my attention, and each of them was a revisit to the tragedy, an uncovering of the wound.

In the midst of my excitement for Sheila and Steve, there was the thought that filled the atmosphere that it would be a sad, undeniable element in the whole celebration. It would have helped to have someone thoughtful enough to include him on the graduation list. It was sad for me that Gene was removed from the yearbook and never mentioned. At the graduation ceremony, as names were called alphabetically by last name of graduates to come forward to receive their certificate, I was overcome with sadness and weeping that Gene was not one of them. It was not fair to Sheila or Steve, but grief was still overshadowing my emotions.

I weep now, but it is not a cry of loneliness or desperation, it is a cry of trust in the God whose comfort always exceeds what He allows His children to go through.

A few months after Sheila and Steve graduated from High School, they decided it was time for them to leave the nest and individually begin their own life-journey. Sheila wanted to go to work to make her own living and moved into an apartment in town with a friend. Steve remained home, went on to College and applied for work to finance his studies, as we were unable to do. After a year or so his school schedule no longer allowed him to keep his job and he decided to join the Air Force to complete his education.

I was sad about not having the children at home any longer but so thankful that God had given my husband back to me to love again and have him to lean on for support and strength. We attended church regularly and tried to become better Christians by taking advantage of every opportunity offered by the church that might be of help in that pursuit. One of those offerings was in the form of a six-month training program regarding maturing in Christ. Assignments included scripture memory, disciplines in prayer and devotion, witnessing, sermon preparation and character development.

Mastering a Bad Habit through *MasterLife*

I felt it was time for me to have a closer walk with Jesus and enrolled in the study offered by my church, entitled *MasterLife*. During my Bible reading time, I came to two verses that brought such conviction to me that I knew I had to change the way I was living to please my Savior. The verses read,

*... Do you not know that your body is the temple of the
Holy Spirit who is in you, whom you have from God,
and you are not your own? For you were bought
at a high price; therefore, glorify God in your body and in
your spirit, which are God's.*

1 Corinthians 6:19-20

At this time I was a heavy smoker and found myself at the point where I felt I could not kick that habit. I had tried before and miserably failed. I faced the fact that I was actually deeply addicted to nicotine and to the habit. These two verses hit me like a ton of bricks. I realized that I was defiling the body that no longer belonged to me but to Christ. In my reasoning, I must be frank to tell you that when I saw church deacons smoking cigarettes right at the entrance to the sanctuary, taking one long, last draw and throwing them down, stomping on what was left with their feet, I had some problem with my thinking process. Had I been looking for an excuse, this would have been enough to justify my continuing with this nasty habit, but I was not looking for an excuse; I was resolved to please God. I had to quit, and eventually, I would. I now realized that I was not honoring God with my action. The next few nights when I went to bed, I told the Lord that the next morning I would not light a cigarette, but my breakfast consisted of both coffee and a cigarette. I was in a double bondage. Then this strategic morning came. The next morning I made myself a cup of coffee, and before I knew it, I had again lit a cigarette. This dread protocol continued for about a week.

I then realized that I was not only addicted to nicotine but to the habit of reaching for and lighting that cigarette. I just knew I had to quit! But how could I? I knew I was hooked, and I could not unhook myself. I was helpless. Then one day when I was all by myself at home, I decided to get on my knees and pray until I had the assurance that God had taken away all my desires pertaining to smoking. After about thirty minutes or so of praying, all of a sudden I was overcome with nausea and followed through with the common result of nausea. I tried to suppress and continue to pray, but it did not work. One can only imagine the rest of the mess. I was then actually scared to continue to pray because I so deeply hated the feelings of nausea and the after effects. So I told God that I had really tried but had miserably failed. Though I desperately wanted to quit smoking, I just could not do it. How to pull this off was now up to Him. I was through trying. The next move was up to Him. I was ready anytime He was.

My husband and I had joined the Winter Bowling League that lasted from September through April the following year. Because it was a church league and none of us were interested in buying alcoholic drinks, we had to take the late shift that usually ended around 11:30 PM. During all those months, I set my alarm for the next morning and had no problem hearing it to get to work on time. On the last night of this particular bowling season, I had set my alarm as usual for six AM, an alarm I never heard. God, in His mercy, had allowed me to miss an alarm to awaken to a new world. When I did awake, my only thoughts were about preparing myself for the day and getting to work on time. I jumped out of bed, rushed through my morning routine of getting ready, ran out of the house and jumped into the car. When I arrived at work, something was very unusual as a whole company of soldiers was waiting to request new identification cards as somehow they had managed to lose theirs over the weekend. This kept my employees so busy that I stepped in and issued cards myself. After the last person had been serviced, I told my employees that I am going to the break area to have me a cup of coffee and a cigarette since I did not have one all morning. On my way to the break area, I felt something trying to pull me back but could not determine what it was. Then it seemed as if I heard a voice saying, "What are you doing? Why do you think you overslept this morning? I caused you to oversleep and kept your mind focused on getting to work on time so that you would not be able to have time for your cup of coffee and that 'simultaneous' cigarette. Now turn around and throw that cigarette away." I recognized that voice as the still small voice of God speaking to me, turned around and did as I was ordered. You see, obedience is the key to God's powerful work in our lives.

> *... Obedience is better than sacrifice ...*
> 1 Samuel 15:22 NLT

From that very moment thirty years ago I no longer desired to smoke, though my husband continued to do so. From then on I had no further longing for cigarettes. That was my day of freedom! I cannot recall the many times my daughter, Sheila, thanked me and told me how glad she was that I no longer smoked. We have such an awesome and powerful God! If we only give Him the chance to work in our lives and turn our situations over to Him, He will set us free and work on behalf of our best!

As time went on, Sheila and Steve each fell in love and soon married and began their families. It was not long before we were gifted with grandchildren and introduced to the joys of grand parenting. What a thrill! We could not wait to visit our grandchildren who soon became the focus of our lives. Sheila, along with her husband and newly born daughter, lived in our town and had decided to meet us every Saturday morning in a restaurant for breakfast. We could not wait for Saturdays to come so we could hold our precious granddaughter. Later that same year Steve notified us that he and his wife Jennifer were having a child. It turned out to be a boy and the first chance we had, we drove to visit them. Oh, how happy we were! As soon as my husband heard that he had a grandson, he bought a tricycle with a horn to give to our new grandson. Now here was a little fellow that, as yet, could not even walk and my husband, in his excitement, was not even thinking that this little one would have to wait quite a while before he could enjoy that gift.

A Rude Intrusion

When at home, I used to enjoy mowing and manicuring our lawn, plant flowers and tend to them. I saw it as exercise and loved the refreshing smell of freshly mown grass. One day, as I got ready to mow the lawn I asked my husband to move his truck from the front lawn to allow me to cut the grass. When I had finished, he went outside and moved his truck back onto the lawn.

I immediately went to the kitchen and began preparing dinner. When the dinner was ready, I looked for my husband but could not find him anywhere in the house or in the yard. He was nowhere to be found. Remembering that he loved to tinker in the garage, I looked there as well. I was stymied and wondered where in the world my husband had gone. Dinner was cooling, and my husband was nowhere to be found. I searched everywhere, behind the garage, front yard, and back. I began to call for him but no answer came. Then I went back into the house and, as I looked out the window, I saw the truck in the front yard with my husband in it, his body slumped forward and his head resting on the steering wheel. With my heart racing, I ran to the truck, swung open the door and touched him, getting no response at first. He finally responded to my excited inquiry, and I noticed that he was slow of speech, seemed confused and very lethargic, at first not even aware of where he was. I had to help him out of the truck and escorted him into the house and told him that I would take him to the hospital. He was very weak, could barely walk and his skin had turned strangely pale. He made little response and had no resistance to a proposed trip to the hospital. I knew then something was dreadfully wrong.

After arriving at the hospital, they immediately took several tests and discovered that my husband's blood count was very low, and they told me that he needed two pints of blood immediately. As they did not have his Medical Records handy, they asked me for his blood type. I did not know, and he was too lethargic to be able to think straight or give reasonable answers. I went to the vehicle where he kept his "Dog Tags" (Dog Tags is a slang term for the identification tags worn on a chain kept by military personnel. They are primarily used for the identification of dead and wounded soldiers; they have personal information about the soldiers and convey essential basic medical information, such as blood type, history of inoculations and religious preference) to verify his blood type. When I returned with his basic medical information, the examining doctor immediately admitted him and gave him a massive blood transfusion, then took more tests to determine the reason for the blood loss. In the meanwhile, one of the doctors took me aside and asked me what I thought might be wrong with my husband to which I replied that I had no clue whatever. I believe he knew that most likely cancer was involved but wanted to test me as to whether I may have suspicioned such. For two weeks my husband lay in the hospital, and it seemed as if nothing was being done about his condition, neither was I informed of the status of his illness. The stress of waiting took its toll on both of us.

Then one Saturday evening, as I was sitting at my husband's bedside, the doctor came into the room and told me that they had found a tumor. He then also explained that various tests had been done, such as upper and lower endoscopy that revealed nothing. They then performed a magnetic resonance enterography (MRE), which revealed the point of the tumor in the small bowel that was the source of the bleeding. Emergency surgery was necessary and critical. By now it was Saturday and hospital personnel were at minimum staffing on weekends. It was necessary to call in surgeons and nurses to perform the surgery. When the head surgeon arrived, he informed me of the planned procedure for this surgery and that it would take many hours. After about two hours the surgeon and a nurse standing next to him called me aside to inform me that they could not do the planned procedure as was explained to me, but had to close him up again without further surgery. He also informed me that they did an immediate lab test, which revealed the worst of all cancers, in the doctor's raw words, "the bastard of all cancers," leiomyosarcoma of the small bowel, an extremely rare form of gastrointestinal malignancy and difficult to visualize by upper and lower endoscopy. The surgeon then proceeded to tell me that my husband had only three to six months left. I remember asking him what he meant by "only three to six months left." He looked at the nurse; she looked at him, and both of them looked at me without saying another word. That's when it hit me... my husband was dying! I loudly cried out "Oh no!"

I could not believe what I heard the doctor say. It could not be, not my husband, not now! We were still on our honeymoon journey after that miraculous event of his salvation and deliverance from alcohol. My daughter, Sheila, was with me and wanted me to come home with her, but I just needed to be by myself. I had to process through this on my own, and no one could help me, not even my children. I had to have a talk with my Lord without interference.

During all this time I did not hear from our pastor or the deacons with the exception of one who had been diagnosed with bone cancer. Everybody within our congregation knew of my husband's condition, but all seemed to shun me now. My daughter and my best, and seemingly only friend, Charlotte, stood with me at this time. I might also add that it was Charlotte who stood by my side during the tragic loss of my son Gene. I was on a journey for which I was totally unprepared. All our other friends seemed suddenly distant and stayed away. I am sure that the reason for this was that they simply did not know what to say or how to respond to us. Few people know how to respond to dire conditions to which they have never been exposed. The thought of the pending event of death is something they had simply no desire to face or to discuss. It seemed to me that I was almost totally abandoned by everybody but God and at times I even doubted His presence. Isolation added to my fear as I faced the possibilities of a long, terrifying walk through another deep, troubling time in my life!

A Bothering Complication

And after you have suffered for a little while, the God of all grace, who has called you to his eternal glory in Christ, will himself restore, support, strengthen, and establish you.

1 Peter 5:10 NRSV

During the last days of my husband's stay in the hospital, I received a call from a bank regarding non-payment of a loan my husband had made. I had no knowledge of this loan and had to try and get some information from my husband even though he was so ill. He told me where to look for the payment book. After I came home, I went to retrieve it and to my amazement, I found the contract for the loan and noticed that he had put our home, our furniture, appliances and everything that was in the house up as collateral. On the signature line, I noticed that someone had signed my name and immediately recognized it as my husband's handwriting. Underneath the signature, a notary had prepared the document, attesting that I had signed the paper in his presence. I could not believe what I was seeing. My own husband had forged my signature. I felt betrayed, angry, hurt. I had so many emotions and questions running through my mind. Not only am I losing my husband, but I am also losing everything else we had worked for all our lives. Here we were, married for thirty years, and I did not know my husband.

I was in shock and in desperation I called my daughter and my son and told them what their father had done and that I now was without a home, without furniture, and without anything. I would now be a homeless person living under a bridge somewhere! I was in complete disbelief and dejection.

My daughter tried to calm me and told me not to worry about all this and to focus on her dad's and my husband's condition. She would contact an attorney and see what steps could be taken to resolve this situation concerning that mystery loan.

When I went to the hospital to see my husband, I was furious and angry and confronted him about the loan and the signature. He told me that he took out the loan to help his sister pay for his father's funeral who had just recently died. I remembered that he had given me $1,000 to send to his sister in the form of a check to contribute to his father's funeral expenses. He also told me that he knew that I would not agree to borrow money from a lending company, and therefore he did not want me to know that he had taken out a loan. Here he was lying there struggling for his life, and I was thinking about myself. That added more pain to me and made me feel even worthless and ashamed for feeling that way. But I felt I had now no choice but to confront him about the finding I made. He told me that he planned to pay the loan back without me ever finding out and that all would have been well. But it was not to be.

In order for me to keep from losing everything, I was advised to have my husband sign a statement attesting to the fact that he had forged my signature and to make sure that he signed it in front of a notary public to legalize it.

When my husband was out of immediate danger, and doctors did everything they could do, he was released from the hospital and placed under the care of a radiologist for needed treatments. Frequent trips for radiation followed as his condition seemed to worsen. Every day after the radiation treatments my husband wanted me to take him to Wendy's restaurant for a frostee. That lifted my hopes that his condition was improving. However, my hopes were short-lived because after three days he just wanted me to take him home. I was fighting a battle on two fronts, first my husband's serious and worsening condition and second, my own severe financial issue. Sadly, on one those days of radiation treatments I took him to our bank to a notary public to attest to the fact that he had forged my signature on that document and that I had no knowledge of it whatsoever. I felt terrible having to drag my husband to the bank to sign that statement, but what was I to do?

This was Thursday morning, the first day of July. The next day my husband wanted to speak with the radiologist to ask him whether the treatments were doing any good. The nurse informed us that the radiologist had left for the weekend because it was the weekend of Independence Day. By Sunday, the fourth of July, my husband was no longer able to swallow water. That's when I took him back to the hospital where the doctor told me that they would put him on a morphine drip and that he would not leave the hospital alive. That meant that he was not expected to live. I remained with my husband until late that night when the nurses told me I should leave. Less than two hours after I left I received a call from the hospital to come immediately because there was a change in my husband's condition. As soon as I got there, I was informed that he had passed away, and I was no longer able to see him. At that moment, it seemed that my whole world had caved in! As I drove home, I felt all alone in this whole wide world. I felt drained and empty, betrayed and abandoned!

Now I was not only mourning the loss of my husband but also had to battle with attorneys who were trying to prove that I masterminded this whole thing about the loan my husband had arranged! I now had to give testimonies by affidavit and depositions. I was so weary.

Except for my two children, my friend Charlotte and one other church member, no one else seemed to care how I was doing. Steve, who served in the United States Air Force, came home for the funeral and stayed for a week to sort through all his father's belongings. How thankful I was that I did not have to go through all the things he left behind. To this day I don't know what my son got rid of, and honestly, I never asked nor was interested in knowing. It is an awesome gift to have children who will stand by you and support you, especially during times of weakness and loss.

I don't know what I would have done had Steve not been available to help me. Sheila had just given birth to her second child and had a full-time job and therefore was not able to provide the support I needed at that time.

On the day my son left to return to his family, his second son was born while he was driving home and he was not able to be with his wife to witness the birth of his precious son. This added to my grief.

Steve and his wife Jennifer, believers in the presence of God amid all the affairs of life, wanted me to quit work and move in with them because they wanted to take care of me. Since I was now a widow, that sounded good to me because it would have freed me from all worries and allowed me to finally get some rest! Though this offer was tempting to me, I decided to tell them to allow me to continue work, until I could retire. They were not too happy about my decision but relented and trusted my judgment.

While my husband was still living, we used to go out to eat with other couples after Sunday or Wednesday evening church services. Now, I was no longer invited to join them. I felt shunned by my own church family and treated like a stranger and decided to look for another church. As time went on, my desire to attend church grew very dim, even to the point that I wanted to stop going altogether. However, I suppose I had too much religion to quit church altogether!

The days were very lonely and the nights seemed oh, so long! Whenever I came home from work, I found myself saying, "Honey, I'm home"! Only to realize that there was no more "honey" to welcome me home!

Three months after my husband's death while I was sitting at my dining room table I had a vision of my husband standing beside me with a smile on his face. I remember saying "you are back!" and stood up to hug him when suddenly he was gone.

My Personal Bout with the Enemy

About six months after my husband's death, I became ill, and several tests were done to determine the nature of my illness. After the last magnetic resonance imaging (MRI) results came in, I was called into the surgeon's office. The same surgeon that performed my husband's surgery and delivered the grave news about his illness delivered the bad news to me as well. He was very apologetic and told me that the (MRI) revealed a tumor on my liver, and it appeared to be cancerous. He proceeded to schedule me for surgery at Walter Reed Army Medical Center in Maryland. I asked him to schedule me locally as my daughter lived in nearby Columbus and wanted to be there with me. However, the nearest hospital with qualified surgeons was Emory Memorial Hospital in Atlanta, Georgia.

When I told Charlotte, my friend, who attended church with me, she mentioned it to the pastor. During the next Wednesday night prayer meeting, church members prayed for my healing while laying hands on me in obedience to God's Word in James 5:14 that reads:

> *Is anyone among you sick? Let him call for the elders*
> *of the church, and let them pray over him,*
> *anointing him with oil in the name of the Lord.*

When my daughter and I arrived at Emory Hospital in Atlanta, they did their own tests and did not find any sign of cancer. My daughter was ecstatic, but I somehow did not share that excitement with her as my mind had been on joining my husband in eternity. I was glad and thankful because I did not want to endure the pain of recovering from surgery that my husband had endured. I was seized by mixed emotions. I was happy that the cancer was gone, but had disappointment because I did not get to die and see my husband. Here was Jehovah-ROPHE—MY HEALER WHO TOOK THE CANCER AWAY. I was grateful for God's healing but still struggled with feelings of abandonment and sorrow and loneliness!

Events such as I have described on these pages have a way of exposing the spiritual realities in one's life. Amid all the complexities of losing my own son to suicide, my husband to cancer, my own threat of serious illness, and my financial problems, I faced the fact that my walk with God was severely deficient, and my faith level was low indeed. To sum it up, I was a mess with a capital "M!"

Oh, I continued to go to church every time the church doors were open, but my life seemed to become more and more empty. I even changed membership again from one church to another, searching for something that I could not put my finger on but would know it when I found it. I was in the desert of RELIGION and to the point of quitting church altogether. However, the miracle of my own healing gave me the new fortitude to fight the battle of my own financial security at hand.

Now I had to deal with attorneys in order to fight to keep my home. I had to go for depositions and hearings and had to endure the abuse of being accused of masterminding this whole process in order to gain a paltry $1,000. The prosecuting attorney tried to prove that I had gained from that transaction by showing the bank ledger where I had deposited $1,000 at that same time of the loan. He just failed to show that I also had written a check two days later in that same amount to my sister-in-law for the funeral expenses and thereby did not profit, not even one cent. The legal process seemed to take forever, but eventually, I prevailed and was able to keep my home and everything that was listed as collateral for the loan my husband had taken. I felt drained but yet very relieved.

Of course, I had forgiven my husband and was freed from the accusation of betrayal. I am sure that he had no malicious intent and was affected by the pressures of the moment and even, perhaps, his own physical issues. Though deeply offended and disappointed, I was freed from the bondage of my own judgments and no longer felt ill will against my departed husband.

On weekends I went to visit my daughter who had a 2-1/2-year-old daughter and a younger one who was now six months old. I loved taking the two-year-old to the park and feeding the ducks in the pond, sit on the swing with her and later, as her sister got old enough, I took her with me as well. Three years later when my daughter's son was born, I took all three of them in a little wagon with a caboose around the block or to the park. I had the privilege of teaching them how to slide down the slide in the park without fear, pushed them on the swing, having picnics and playing hide and seek, etc. In the winter when it snowed, which rarely happened, I took them to build a snowman. Around Christmas time I took them into the woods and collected pine cones, brought them home and spray painted them white, silver and gold and used them as decoration in the house. As I had opportunity, I flew to where my son's family was stationed and spent time with them who also had children of the same ages.

My work was with the US Military as a civil service worker. Having come to America as a war bride was also not the easiest thing for me. I wondered if I would always be seen as the enemy? I worked with the retirement services and pensions and at times had to fight to ensure my position. There were times military retirees would become irate over a decision that was made way over my head, but I had to implement the decision. I rarely felt like anyone was willing to fight for me, to protect me, to cherish me. I was scared; I was lonely; I was empty! There were times

I wanted to go back home to Germany, but my life wasn't really there anymore. My remaining family was here in the States, and my job and career were here as well. I was in a place of limbo, feeling disconnected, spiritually and physically. "Alone" can be a tormenting, terrifying word when one's spiritual grid is incomplete without a lingering sense of the presence of God. Though I knew full well that I was a child of God and would go to heaven when I died, I had not been taught to know and apply the truths of His presence and provisions. The continuing blows in this season of my life served to expose my weakness of faith and landed me in a position of desperation. I could not go on as usual. I needed something to happen to me, and I would not settle until I found it! I began to be assaulted by questions that demanded answers:

"Does my dissatisfaction with this life and everything that is happening have a purpose in God's plan for me?"

"Could it be that life has been set up by God in such a way that nothing on this earth can fully satisfy us and that sooner or later I may hunger for more than this world has to offer?"

"When is all that has happened to me going to make sense and where was I to look for direction and meaning?"

I found myself at this point! In review of those days, now many years down-line, the words "Quo Vadis" strike me as significant. The words in Latin mean, "Where are you going or where to from here?" I realize that I was facing the remainder of my life and asking, "What now?" The rest of my story is God's massive and undeniable answer to that valid question few ever ask, but all should. Yes, I was asking God, but I was also asking myself, "Where to from here?" The trajectory of my troubled life was about to change. Happily, I leave the past, knowing full well that my troubles and disappointments do not define me. Welcome to the future, compliments of a loving God!

Chapter 7

There Had to be More!

*Surely your goodness and unfailing love will pursue me
all the days of my life,
and I will live in the house of the Lord forever.*
Psalm 23:6 NLT

The preceding chapters have been painful to remember and write but greatly helpful as a source of thanksgiving and praise that I made it through it all. I am sure that it has been therapeutic as well. However, as I sensed a new season coming, I remember feeling rather numb and confused, squarely facing the fact that all indications pointed to the fact that I needed a general spiritual revolution in my life.

The best description I can give of my spiritual status is the following:

"I felt dissatisfied with life, sick of church, without joy, empty, without purpose, and life had become a drag."

Little did I know about how drastic this next season would prove to be. Enjoy the journey with me as we walk through the adventure of God's agenda for one woman's life.

An Old Story

An old book entitled, The Salty Tang, contains several sermons that in an imaginative or fictional setting gives unique meaning to the stories with which we are all familiar. One of the chapters is entitled, *Yes, I Remember Bethlehem*, and features the apostle, Luke, paying a visit to an imaginary fellow named Jesse

Benhadad, the innkeeper who turned Joseph and Mary away but caught himself and granted them the privilege of staying in the stable behind the inn because the inn was full. The event, of course, took place many years before and the innkeeper, now feeble with age, is responding to Luke's question regarding the events and his memory of them. Luke finds that the events have rigidly remained in the old man's mind, and he is filled with wonder that, though he knew something huge was occurring, he hadn't known the rest of the story. Frederick Speakman, the author, puts words in Jesse's mouth that are fetching:

> "Luke, how are you ever going to know life's
> moments when they come? The great hours, the shining
> hours, the ones that later, can mean so much—
> they come walking up like any other hour, and always
> when you're busy. Always when you're convinced what
> you're doing is so important. And you let them go,
> and you never know."

After describing that night with words that give indication that Jesse has been mulling over those moments for all these years of the startled shepherds, the clouds, punctured and leaking music, the sounds of angels' voices, the unexplainable brightness of the light of that remarkable night and his (Jesse) own feeling that something so important was taking place. But he hadn't heard the rest of the story! Luke proceeds to tell him, and the old man responds with glad excitement to the story.

When I heard the story I realized that something like this was happening to me that would matter forever!

My Personal Invitation from God

One day I received a letter from the pastor of the church

I had previously attended. It was an invitation for Spiritual Renewal Services with Leif Hetland.

While reading the letter, I became angry. I really don't know to this day why I was so angry. I said to myself: "Who does that pastor think he is, insinuating that I am not living right?" On top of that, now he is getting fancy, calling it "spiritual renewal" instead of revival. Evidently, something was really brewing within me. We had annual revival services with guest speakers but never "spiritual renewal." It was just something different but I never really sensed the Holy Spirit during these revival meetings. In retrospect, I now know that, to me, it was a matter of word-usage. We call certain experiences by acceptable names when, as a matter of fact, it doesn't add up to essential identity. We call the small storage area in our automobile to the right of the driver a "glove compartment" and seldom, if ever, find gloves there. We call a period of time "the good old days" when upon closer examination, they weren't so good after all. The fact is, the farther we get from them, the better they look. Ages ago we got accustomed to having a few days of "protracted meetings" and labeled the experience "revival" when, in fact, most of the time, at best, they amounted to little more than a fever followed by a chill. Well, I had become acclimatized to Church terminology without ever examining the meaning of the terms. So when I was confronted by this new term "spiritual renewal" I was offended. Frankly, had I been asked why, I could not have given a reasonable answer. I had experienced a few so-called "revivals" and had never thought to define what was meant by the term. All I knew was that there were more meetings closer together, often a full week or more. The singing and preaching seemed louder and longer, and the atmosphere was more upbeat and more excited. If one was going to get saved, the "revival" seemed like an ideal time to experience it. But when it was over, everything was back to "normal" with the exception that we were very tired from the long and loud series of meetings at the church.

There I was, confronted by a strange new term "spiritual renewal." I started to tear up the letter and just forget about it. But somehow I was not able to do it, and I just tossed it to the other end of my table.

A few days later I picked up that letter and read it again and this time I felt something that I could not explain. I was overcome with conviction regarding my spiritual status, so I told God that I could not go on living the way I was. You see I was very unhappy. I had no desire for worship, no desire to talk to people and I had become a bitter and angry person. After I read the letter again, I told God, "Okay Lord, I will go but when I go, I need for You to show up. And if You show up, don't pass me by!" To be honest, I am not sure what I meant by what I said. Had I been asked what I meant by this prayer I surely would have admitted that, to be honest, I didn't have a clue! What did I mean by "God showing up" or by the statement, "don't pass me by?" Did God just do a number on me and put those words in my mouth that He most wanted to hear? Frankly, now that I am writing about the experience, I find myself believing that this is exactly what He did! He was simply and sovereignly answering his own prayer. The next evening I drove myself to the Church where all this was taking place. I don't know what I was expecting, but I can assure you that what I saw did not fit my theology of God's presence. I heard this man with a strange accent preach a message that strangely touched me but when he presented the invitation for people to respond, what happened suddenly offended my religious senses. Leif Hetland, a Norwegian, the guest preacher for the "Spiritual Renewal," had a remarkable delivery and unique approach to personal ministry. My mind simply could not make sense of what was happening. I suppose most of us have heard the adage, "we are generally down on what we are not up on." Well, I certainly reacted to these "new" events. As I was watching from my comfortable position near the back of the Church, people were walking to the front in response to the preacher's invitation and instead of shaking their hands and directing them to sit down, he seemed to touch them, and they fell flat on the floor. I thought, "This is not of God; this has to be the enemy! I don't even do this in my own house. This is just not right!" The sight of these people falling to the floor in the house of God was more than I could stand. My refined religious feelings were offended, so I promptly stood up, turned on my heels, walked out of the Church, got in my car and drove home. A bit angry, somewhat mystified, mildly offended, decidedly disappointed, I prepared for what I thought would be a good night of rest without even trying to process the events of the evening. I went to bed rather shocked and somewhat numb.

As I had to get up early the next morning to go to work, I intended to get several hours of sleep, but sleep would not come. I may have momentarily dozed off and, if so, I was almost immediately awakened. I don't know whether I was dreaming or not, but my mind was racing. It seemed to me that God was speaking to me by asking pointed questions for which I had no answers but the word, "Yes."

The conversation went something like this:

God: "Did I not hear you say that you no longer liked the way you felt about yourself or people and did not want to go on living the way you were living?"

Friede: "Yes."

God: "Did I not also hear you say that you would go to the spiritual renewal services?"

Friede: "Yes."

God: "Did I not also hear you say that you wanted me to show up?"

Friede: "Yes."

God: "Did I not also hear you say that if you came, you did not want Me to pass you by?"

Friede: "Yes."

God: "I did show up as you requested and I saw you. But you did not give me the opportunity to pass you by. You ran out on Me. If you ever ask Me anything again, you better mean it or don't waste My time!"

End of conversation! I started to weep bitterly because I realized that I had grieved my Lord and He, the Creator of the whole cosmos, visited me in the night and talked with me. I realized that He was pursuing me all along even when I did not realize it. He was working behind the scenes, proactive in the circumstances of my life, bringing me to a place where through His grace I could experience Him. Writing this, I am overcome with emotions about how much God loves us that He will stop at nothing to bring us to Himself.

For God so loved the world that He gave His only begotten
Son, that whoever believes in Him should not perish
but have everlasting life.

John 3:16

I asked the Lord to forgive me for not recognizing His Presence and for mistaking Him as the enemy. I also asked Him to please come again the next evening and promised Him I would wait for Him and not run out on Him.

The next evening, as Leif was ministering, he spoke on the Pearl of Great Price. I had never heard anything like it and didn't want the message to end. I felt God's pull on my heart, drawing me ever closer to Himself. On the basis of my conversation with God the night before, I knew that I had to respond to the invitation. When Leif finished the message and gave the invitation, I arose from my seat and walked up to him and told him that I wanted the Pearl of Great Price about Whom he spoke. The moment he prayed, I had an incredible experience with God. That moment I felt God come all over me. I felt such a love and peace as I had never known before.

God met me head-on and quickened my Spirit. He lighted a fire within me that is still burning. It is difficult, even now, to put into words. I cannot describe it, but all my desires, my emotions, and my thoughts were changed. The Holy Spirit changed my life forever in one moment!

All I wanted from that moment on was to be with the Lord, to be in His presence, to know Him, to love him and to serve Him, whatever that meant. It was the first time in my life that I knew what it was to desire God and to get to truly know Him. I had fallen head over heals in love with Jesus and suddenly became aware that I was not alone. Jesus had taken my departed husband's place, filled me with a sense of His presence and was now my constant companion. He now had become my husband.

For your Maker is your husband, the Lord of hosts is His name; and your Redeemer is the Holy One of Israel; He is called the God of the whole earth.

Isaiah 54:5

The Bible suddenly became alive to me and I could feel God's tangible, manifest presence in my everyday life. I wanted to share the love I felt with others. I began to experience an intimate relationship with Jesus Christ. I had become so hungry for His presence that I went searching for meetings where Leif may be ministering because he carried the presence of Jesus in such a powerful way. I thought in order to be used by Jesus I needed what Leif had – the anointing that I had never seen before. I had become like Elisha who wanted a double portion of the Prophet Elijah's anointing. Three times Elijah told Elisha to stay in a certain city, while he, Elijah, was going on. Three times Elisha refused to stay and said:

As the Lord lives, and as you yourself live, I will not leave you.
2 Kings 2:2, 4, & 6

I was so hungry for the things of the Holy Spirit. One evening I went to one of those meetings where I had a powerful encounter with the Holy Spirit. While driving home at the speed limit on the Interstate shortly before midnight, I did not notice a car behind me driving at high speed without lights until the driver rear-ended me with such force that my car was moved several yards forward. When I realized what had happened, the other driver had swerved into to other lane and taken the exit and was gone into the night. When the Police arrived, they asked me where I had been and whether I had been drinking. I found that very odd, especially since I was the one being "hit" by the other car. That impact severely damaged my car, but thankfully I was not hurt whatsoever. I believe there were two elements involved:

1. The devil was not happy with my desire and hunger for more of God.
2. Angels were present to keep the enemy from attacking my physical body.

A few weeks later, during our Wednesday night prayer meeting, my pastor played a CD about the Father's Love. It so wrecked me and shook my whole inner being that I was completely undone and wept intensely. In that instant, I experienced the love of Father God that is out of this world and unexplainable. He has become the Father to me that I always longed for but never knew, and I wanted to know Him more and more! It was so powerful and overwhelming that no matter how much time has passed, it continues to have such a grip on me that I cannot escape. It saturates my entire being. I believe that at that moment God began to launch me into the destiny He had for me as His child! Following are the lyrics of that CD by Father Heart Communications. I encourage you to read them slowly and allow them to speak to you as well.

Father's Love Letter

My Child,

You may not know me, but I know everything about you (Psalm 139:1).

I know when you sit down and when you rise up (Psalm 139:2).

I am familiar with all your ways (Psalm 139:3).

Even the very hairs on your head are numbered (Matthew 10:29-31).

For you were made in my image (Genesis 1:27).

In me, you live and move and have your being (Acts 17:28) .

For you are my offspring (Acts 17:28).

I knew you even before you were conceived (Jeremiah 1:4-5).

I chose you when I planned creation (Ephesians 1:11-12).

You were not a mistake, for all your days are written in my book (Psalm 139:15-16).

I determined the exact time of your birth and where you would live (Acts 17:26).

You are fearfully and wonderfully made (Psalm 139:14).

I knit you together in your mother's womb (Psalm 139:13).

And brought you forth on the day you were born (Psalm 71:6).

I have been misrepresented by those who don't know me (John 8:41-44).

I am not distant and angry but am the complete expression of love (1 John 4:16).

And it is my desire to lavish my love on you (1 John 3:1).

Simply because you are my child, and I am your Father (1 John 3:1).

I offer you more than your earthly father ever could (Matthew 7:11).

For I am the perfect father (Matthew 5:48).

Every good gift that you receive comes from my hand (James 1:17).

For I am your provider, and I meet all your needs (Matthew 6:31-33).

My plan for your future has always been filled with hope (Jeremiah 29:11).

Because I love you with an everlasting love (Jeremiah 31:3).

My thoughts toward you are countless as the sand on the seashore (Psalm 139:17-18).

And I rejoice over you with singing (Zephaniah 3:17).

I will never stop doing good to you (Jeremiah 32:40).

For you are my treasured possession (Exodus 19:5).

I desire to establish you with all my heart and all my soul (Jeremiah 32:41).

And I want to show you great and marvelous things (Jeremiah 33:3).

If you seek me with all your heart, you will find me (Deuteronomy 4:29).

Delight in me and I will give you the desires of your heart (Psalm 37:4).

For it is I who gave you those desires (Philippians 2:13).

I am able to do more for you than you could possibly imagine (Ephesians 3:20).

For I am your greatest encourager (2 Thessalonians 2:16-17).

I am also the Father who comforts you in all your troubles (2 Corinthians 1:3-4).

When you are brokenhearted, I am close to you (Psalm 34:18).

As a shepherd carries a lamb, I have carried you close to my heart (Isaiah 40:11).

One day I will wipe away every tear from your eyes (Revelation 21:3-4).

And I'll take away all the pain you have suffered on this earth (Revelation 21:3-4).

I am your Father, and I love you even as I love my son, Jesus (John 17:23).

For in Jesus, my love for you is revealed (John 17:26).

He is the exact representation of my being (Hebrews 1:3).

He came to demonstrate that I am for you, not against you (Romans 8:31).

And to tell you that I am not counting your sins (2 Corinthians 5:18-19).

Jesus died so that you and I could be reconciled (2 Corinthians 5:18-19).

His death was the ultimate expression of my love for you (1 John 4:10).

I gave up everything I loved that I might gain your love (Romans 8:31-32).

If you receive the gift of my son Jesus, you receive me (1 John 2:23).

And nothing will ever separate you from my love again (Romans 8:38-39).

Come home and I'll throw the biggest party heaven has ever seen (Luke 15:7).

I have always been Father, and will always be Father (Ephesians 3:14-15).

My question is ... Will you be my child (John 1:12-13)?

I am waiting for you (Luke 15:11-32).

**Love, Your Dad
Almighty God**

(Love Letter is a compilation of paraphrased Bible verses presented in the form of a love letter from God to you. ©Father's 1999, Father Heart Communications, FathersLoveLetter.com.)

I was elated that I was discovering, at last, that I had a Father who really cared for me, knew everything about me and was with me all the time. During the next days I attended a Father's Heart Conference in Atlanta, Georgia with Jack Frost who spoke about forgiving our fathers whether they were dead or alive. Then and there, after hours of struggle, I forgave my father and realized that he could not give love because he had none to give, even for himself. We cannot give what we do not have!

As the awareness grew that I was in the family of God, I began to have experiences that were living proof of the fact that my Father knew where I was and had already made arrangements for my care. I was not accustomed to feeling the love of a father since my own father made it known that he did not love me, value me or care for me.

Learning to Live with God's Care

From this point on my life was no longer mundane or ordinary. Things started happening that were not possible in the natural. If you would have offered me a million dollars to go back to the days before Christ revealed Himself to me that night through the power of His Holy Spirit, I would tell you to keep your million dollars; I'd rather have Christ in me Who is the hope of glory! I'd rather walk in love, joy, peace, patience, kindness, goodness, faith, meekness, and self-control. He is all I ever wanted; He is all I ever needed. A tree that does not bear fruit is a dead tree. I want to live and make a difference in this world. I want to experience life the way God has intended for us to live. I want to be a fruit bearer!

By this My Father is glorified, that you bear much fruit; so you will be My disciples.

John 15:8

Shortly after I began to experience life in the Spirit and fell head over heels in love with Jesus, one night I was attacked in my sleep. I felt that I was being choked. From the nature of the attack, I was virtually sure that it was a demon, and I also knew that in order to overcome him I had to let him know that Jesus was my defender. However, at this moment I could barely think the name of Jesus, much less speak it, because of my shortness of breath. I was in spiritual warfare and realized that until I could say "Jesus," I was headed toward defeat. Though I was near panic and almost breathless, I continued the fight. I knew I had a battle on my hands and had to stand my ground. It was a long, hard fight until I was able to say "J," continuing my pursuit to freedom, I did not give up until I was able to say "Je-" and then that wonderful name came across my lips, "Jesus!" As soon as I said that name, the demon was gone and immediately I was able to breathe normally again. The rest of the night was filled with blessed peace. I will never forget that night because it was precisely the time I realized the awesome power that was in the name of Jesus.

"Jesus, Jesus, Jesus,
There's just something about that Name.
Master, Savior, Jesus,
Like the fragrance after the rain.

139

Jesus, Jesus, Jesus,
Let all heaven and earth proclaim,
Kings and kingdoms will all pass away,
But there's something about that Name."

Gloria Gaither

I thought some really strange things were happening with my mind. I didn't truly understand visions or dreams and had not thought of the possibility that God would give me either one.

On one occasion, when I was driving from Columbus, Georgia to Tampa, Florida, I experienced a tire blowout on the right front of my car. I was driving in the center lane on Interstate I-75. I had a phone available in my car, but I could not call for help. I knew that the first question would be, "What is your location?" I also knew that I would have no answer because I did not realize where I was. I had been listening to worship music and praying and singing and never paid any attention to whether I was still in Georgia or had already crossed the state line into Florida. I didn't even know which exit I had passed. With the traffic very heavy, heading toward Florida, I asked God to clear one of the outer lanes for me to get me out of the center lane. Looking into my rear view mirror, I noticed the left lane was completely clear, allowing me to just cruised into the median. There I sat, not anxious about anything but just telling Jesus that, as my husband, I would trust him to get me to Tampa somehow that day. Immediately after saying that, a State Highway Patrolman pulled up in front of me. The officer got out of his car and walked up to my window to inquire about my situation. I explained to him what had just happened. My right tire had blown out a minute before. He promptly turned back toward his cruiser and shortly returned with a triangular caution sign directing traffic around us. He removed his floor mat from his cruiser and placed it by the blown out tire. He also asked me whether I had a lug wrench and a car jack. I unpacked the Christmas gifts that filled the trunk of the car and handed him the lug wrench and the small car-jack that he used to remove the blown out tire and install the little spare tire we call the "donut." The officer began to leave, and I asked him to wait a minute and reached among the gifts to retrieve a little box of chocolate-covered macadamia nuts. He didn't want to accept the gift, but I insisted, and he complied with profuse gratitude. He then asked me to follow him to the next exit and instructed me to get help at the nearest tire place. While I owed the kind patrolman my thanks, I knew that he was simply being used as God's instrument to reassure me that He always provides for His Own.

On another occasion, I was left stranded once again, but this time, when I pressed the gas pedal, it seemed as if no fuel went to the engine and my car started slowing down. Once again, I was in the center lane and traffic in the left and the right lanes was moving fast. I prayed for God to clear the right lane, which He did immediately! I could just simply coast from the center lane to the right side. There I was again, continuing to praise and worship with assurance that my God was in control and knew my situation and would send help. Being in total peace and perfect contentment, I suddenly noticed a State Highway Patrol car next to me! I told the officer of my dilemma. He called for a wrecker to pull my car into the next exit with a service station that had a mechanic on duty. The officer followed me to ensure my safety. When I arrived at the station, they found the problem to be a faulty fuel pump and informed me that they did not have one on hand but could get one at another place located fifty miles away. They also told me they were closing at noon, which was within the hour, as it was Saturday and I would have to leave the car with them and wait until Monday. I explained to them that I was on my way to Tampa and that my grandchildren were expecting me. The person in charge told me then that someone would take me to the local restaurant for lunch while they would get the fuel pump and repair the car. Would you believe that three hours later I was on my way! Don't ask me how they did all this in such a short time or why they were willing to work past closing time. The only explanation I have for that is my heavenly Father's favor and kindness!

These events marked the beginning of such happenings that would continue to reveal the measure of the Father's love and care for the rest of my life. It was just the beginning of the wonderful work of the Holy Spirit in my life.

A New Opportunity to Serve my Father

I became aware that what had happened to me involved far more than God just taking care of me. I had a passion to reciprocate with thanksgiving and return, at least in part, the favor He was showing me. Thus I was ready when the first opportunity came my way.

Leif Hetland, who had been used of God to acquaint me with God as my loving husband, a few months earlier, had planned a mission's trip to Africa. Leif was Missions Pastor of a local church in Georgia and periodically led mission trips to foreign countries. He had planned a trip to Mozambique and was talking about the journey while speaking in the church I was attending. He stated that the mission had been planned, the group was being formed, and everybody was welcome. He specified that age made no difference and that anyone who knew Jesus was qualified. I was surprised that I felt a real desire, in fact, a burning in my heart, to go on this trip. So, a while later, I found myself in a small group led by Leif on our way to Mozambique! Once in the country, during an outdoor crusade, we began praying for people. Nothing out of the ordinary seemed to be happening, but I was enjoying being involved in world missions!

While praying for one woman I was unaware of anything unusual happening; that is, visually or emotionally. However, I was feeling a measure of what I would have recognized as the anointing. The next evening an usher came to me and wanted me to accompany him to the back of the platform of the outdoor crusade where two sisters were waiting for me. The usher explained to me that one of them was deaf from childhood, and God had opened her right ear after I prayed with her the night before. Now she wanted me to pray with her again for God to open her other ear. I prayed, and her other ear was opened. Hallelujah! So I was in the midst of "on-the-job-training," I was learning as I went along. One thing I learned was that God does not always reveal to us the manner and magnitude of what He is doing when we are ministering. Something else I realized was that God delights in showing off and showing out through us, for it is the *"Christ in us, the hope of glory!"* How exciting is that? And that did me in! That's what I call the abundant life! That, to me, is what life is all about.

> *And these signs will follow those who believe:*
> *In My name, they will cast out demons;*
> *they will speak with new tongues …*
> *they will lay hands on the sick,*
> *and they will recover.*
> Matthew 16:17-18

This all happened while I was working at my regular job at Fort Benning, Georgia. At the beginning of each year, we had to submit our request for annual leave or vacation time for the remainder of the year. When I requested, on short notice, a ten-day vacation in the fall to go on another mission trip, my superior rather quickly approved it. Other employees noticed this and complained because they had to submit their requests early in the year and he had approved mine spontaneously upon my request. His reply to their complaint was simply, "She is working for a higher power than me!" I sat there with mouth wide open and tears flowing down my cheeks, thinking, "What is God doing? How is this possible?"

God can do anything, you know—far more than you could ever imagine or guess or request in your wildest dreams! He does it not by pushing us around but by working within us, his Spirit deeply and gently within us.

Ephesians 3:20 MSG

Changing Employers

One day Leif Hetland asked me if I would handle the financial records of his newly-established missions organization, Global Mission Awareness, informing me that it would only require about two or three hours a week. I thought to myself that I could do this on weekends because during the week I was too occupied with my full-time job. I told him that though I had been the treasurer at my church, I had no experience with a 501c3 organization. He replied that, in this case, we would learn together and he handed me his checkbook and said, "Here, take care of this!" I was shocked and in disbelief and said, "What if I were to run away with this?" He replied, "I don't care. It is not my money; it is God's!" That day God showed me something about Himself. He showed me that, though we don't know much about His business or His Kingdom, He trusts us to take care of it and be His representatives.

Things at my regular job with the government began to change. I was doing well, but my heart was no longer in my work. Jesus had stolen my heart and changed my desires. I loved doing mission work, so I decided to retire early and join Leif's mission organization on a full-time basis.

I realized that I was being introduced to a new level of living, learning to listen to the voice of God. I was finding out that, once a child of His is willing, He begins to open opportunities for service.

My pastor ministered at two nursing homes in our town. One day He asked me to come with him. During his ministry to the patients, he asked me to come up front and say a word to the precious elderly people. I had no clue as to what to say, but I greeted them and told them that God loved them. That is always appropriate and true! Then the Lord gave me a greater hunger for His Word. One day the Pastor could not go to the nursing home and asked me to go and take his place. I was scared out of my wits. But God's grace was sufficient, and He gave me a message for the patients. He said, "Just tell them, 'Remember Lot's wife!'" Not knowing what that was all about, I did some prayerful research and shared what I felt God was revealing to me. God trusted me with the secrets of His heart to reach His people! I was humbled and overwhelmed. How could He use this broken, weary immigrant to touch the hearts of His people? Then I realized that God always uses the broken and the weak, always using our negatives to reveal His positives. All He needs and wants is our willingness and commitment. Happily, He does the rest!

But we have this treasure in jars of clay to show that this all-surpassing power is from God and not from us.
2 Corinthians 4:7 NIV

My grace is sufficient for you, for my power is made perfect in weakness. Therefore I will boast all the more gladly about my weaknesses so that Christ's power may rest on me.
2 Corinthians 12:9 NIV

I had never experienced anything like this! While I shared the love of Jesus with these frail, sick and elderly people, God touched them. Some began to weep! Others gave their lives to Jesus, and still, others wanted to have a closer walk with Jesus and were experiencing His healing power.

God was preparing me for a new level of ministry. He showed me that in the process of life we need to apply faith and trust in Jesus, and He makes it such a joy to become more intimate with Him. I fell head over heals in love with Jesus even more than ever.

An Early Problem in the Ministry

My daughter and I had always been best friends. After my spiritual awakening, she seemed gradually to have less and less to do with me. She was not accustomed to her mother's new way of life and soon wanted nothing to do with me. We went from best friends to total strangers. I was hurt and tried to do whatever it took to keep our relationship alive. I knew what it would take—I would have had to stop following God as passionately as I did and quit going on mission trips to foreign countries because of the inherent dangers involved for single women.

I did not realize at that time that what was happening to me was common fare for those who really had decided to yield totally to Jesus. There is a hymn we used to sing, "I Have Decided to Follow Jesus" and it became my anthem. There was simply no turning back for me. I wouldn't be like Lot's wife, looking back to a life without God's blessing or provision. I loved my daughter and grandchildren but refused to quit following my God! It was a hard choice, but I did it! I was learning now the meaning of the words of Paul in Acts 14:22b,

We must through many tribulations
enter the kingdom of God.

When I insisted on going on one of these trips, she tried to discourage me, speaking of the dangers a single woman faced in a foreign country. She saw that I was determined and could not be dissuaded, and it angered her severely. As a result, our relationship became more and more estranged and distant.

In the year 2003, Leif told me that he and his family were moving to Florence, Alabama and they wanted me to move as well. I told him that I just could not leave my family. Besides that, my late husband brought me to this town, and we had our home here all those years. It was the only place in America I had ever lived and felt a sense of loyalty toward him even though he had already been deceased for ten years. Leif was so gracious to let me work in the office in Columbus even after his move. However, the saying "out of sight out of mind" became a reality financially. People and churches stopped supporting the ministry, and Leif had to close the Columbus office. That meant I had to make a decision whether to move and work at his new office in Alabama or stay in Columbus without close contact to Leif and the family. So as I dealt with this decision whether to leave or stay, God led me to the story of Elijah and Elisha. Elijah requested that Elisha change his profession and make the life-altering decision to terminate his work on his farm, offering his oxen as sacrifices to God and burning his farm instruments. I was not following the man, Leif Hetland or his organization, Global Mission Awareness, but in my heart, I was following the anointing of God that I saw in both Leif and on the organization.

Before making a final decision regarding such a drastic move, I called my daughter and asked for a meeting with her. I knew that what she had to say would have a bearing on this crucial decision in my life. When she consented to meeting, she insisted that we meet at her house. I agreed to such a meeting, and the first words out of my mouth were, "You have built a wall between us and I can no longer climb over it." Her reply was quick and firm, "That's right, and the wall will stay." My heart was crushed. "In that case," I said to her, "I have nothing left in this town, and I might as well move." Her reply was very short, "OK!" For me, the decision was settled.

Though I could not believe what was happening, the event, as painful as it was, made clearer the nature of the opportunity of pursuing my relationship to Jesus. That sealed my decision to continue to follow what I believed to be my destiny.

I am convinced today that God graciously used my precious daughter's issues about our relationship to further His agenda. Proof of this to me is the wonderful state of our present relationship as I write these words. As I look back, I now know that God had far more in mind for me than I could ever have imagined. Though I loved my Georgia family and remembered Georgia as the only place I had lived for forty years, I was willing to choose God's will over every other consideration. As difficult as it was, I now realize it was a key factor in bringing me to where I now happily find myself at this moment.

No sooner than my decision was settled, I was asked the question by someone in Florence, "Are you going to move?" I quickly said, "Yes!" At that very moment, I experienced such a sharp pain in my lower back that I felt like I could not walk. In a later diagnosis, my physician cited a bulging disk and a sciatic nerve as the source of the pain. I wondered about the timing of this event. Why at the very moment of my affirmative answer to the question regarding my impending move had the severe pain occurred? On recounting the experience, I believe God allowed the enemy to inflict the pain in order to confirm the rightness of the move. A similar Old Testament story seems fitting here. When Joseph finally identified himself after many years to his brothers who had sold him into slavery, he calmed their fears by saying:

*But as for you, you planned evil against me; but God meant it
for good, in order to bring it about as it is this day,
to save many people alive.*

Genesis 50:20

I am not sure that this was a revelation from God, but I certainly considered it a favorable possibility, a position I still hold. If so, God does not stop with just getting the point across; thus we must not stop there either. The fact that God uses a painful experience to His and our advantage may tell us more than we think we need to know at the time. As we keep our spiritual eyes open, we may see later that we learned more than was previously recognized. I went through the process of chiropractic adjustments, prescriptions for pain and physical therapy with no improvement whatsoever. Though the doctor in charge recommended surgery as the final solution, I refused that option immediately on the basis of a prophetic word from a stranger. The treatment protocol followed for several weeks involved the conviction that the prophetic word was accurate. In addition my relentless belief in the impending healing and my repeated confession each time I was questioned, "I am walking out my healing," served as vital components in my treatment. Within weeks amid this protocol, one day I suddenly recognized that my pain was gone! I had been healed! My severe back problem was a thing of the past!

My next move was to call a realtor to list my home in Columbus for sale. After four months of waiting for the sale of my house, Leif informed me of his desire to close the Columbus office and open his Alabama office on March 1, 2004. I packed two suitcases, and at the invitation of Leif and Jennifer moved into their home. I might add, with a great deal of pleasure, that their four charming children kindly received me as a member of the family. While there, I worked at the new office and began looking for a permanent home for myself.

I had no idea what was next. On my way to my new destination, the Lord reminded me of the message I gave at the nursing home concerning Lot's wife. Not knowing what that was all about, He told me that the word He had given me then was really meant for me now. I was not to look back for any reason! The move to Alabama was more than just a geographical event; it was a total change of life from fear to faith and from reason to revelation. I was learning to live what Jesus called

> *... not living by bread alone*
> *but by every word from the mouth of God.*
>
> Luke 4:4

Another significant scripture came to me that further enlightened my journey:

> *"I tell you the truth," Jesus said to them, "no one who has left home or wife or brothers or parents or children for the sake of the Kingdom of God will fail to receive many times as much in this age and, in the age to come, eternal life."*
>
> Luke 18:29-30 NIV

More of God's Care

> *The thief does not come except to steal, and to kill, and to destroy. I have come that they may have life and that they may have it more abundantly.*
>
> John 10:10

When I was getting ready to put my house on the market to sell in 2004 for the move from Columbus, GA to Florence, Alabama I found it infested with termites. I did have a contract with a nationally well-known termite/pest control company who I had contracted ten years earlier with continuing annual inspections. Three months after their last inspection, at which time they told me that all was clear, the room that had been built as an addition to the house was infested with termites from the front of the house all the way across the top to the bottom of the back of the house.

When I notified the termite company and asked the manager to come and look at this, he came and told me that he was sorry but that they were not responsible to pay me for the damages because I did not have the contract that required them to pay for damages should there be any. I told him the reason I did not sign that particular contract was that I assumed that, if they did their job, there should not be any damage. I had gotten an estimate for repairs, which required completely tearing out all the ruined wood and rebuilding the room from scratch, an estimate of $6,000.

Friends recommended I hire an attorney and take the company to court. An independent pest control company owner, who was an attorney, also recommended that I do so. Based on the company not doing their job accurately, he felt I could win the case even though I did not sign the contract for them to pay for damages. But somehow I felt I did not have permission from the Lord to do so and did not file suit. I told the Lord at that time that I felt it was not fair, it was not right that they should get away with failing to do their job and still taking my money. That's when He led me to Exodus 14:14 (NLT) where he told Moses:

The LORD himself will fight for you. Just stay calm.

I took that as a promise from God to me and did not hire an attorney.

After I had the repairs done, I went to a conference with Leif. When I returned, I had a voicemail on my phone to contact the Termite Company. They then told me that they were not obligated to pay for the damages, "however, we want to do the right thing." That shocked me! They offered to pay me half the amount of the estimate I had given them with the stipulation that they would no longer cover my house. I really did not care since I was trying to sell it anyway.

End result: The actual cost of repairs was $3,500 for which they paid all but $500. Had I hired an attorney; I believe I would have lost the case because the law has no grace.

I like telling this story, not to brag on me but to brag on God. I knew that according to scripture, He was a Father to the orphans and a Husband to the widows, so I took Him at His word.

Does God keep His promises? You bet!

Approximately three months after I went to Florence to stay with Leif and Jennifer and their children, I found what I thought was the perfect house for me and signed the contract to buy it. I did not make that decision based on my resources but based on God's resources. I did not have sufficient funds, not even for a down payment, as my house in Columbus had not sold yet. You may call it irresponsible; I call it supernatural, especially since I was able to make a down payment, sign the contract for a fifteen-year payoff and then doubled the monthly mortgage to have the house paid off within seven and one-half years. After choosing flooring and counter tops and appliances, I moved in, bringing all my belongings from Columbus, Georgia to my new home in Alabama where I thought I would now live for the rest of my life. I had so much fun fixing up the house just like I wanted it. Leif's wife, Jennifer, and I really had some good times working on projects together. We were walking through Lowe's looking for something one day and she said, "Friede, that guy was totally checking you out!" I had not noticed and replied, "Oh really?" I was so in love with Jesus that I really had not thought anything about romance in my life. I thought, "been there, done that."

Let me reiterate that I was happily situated with Jesus; He was everything in my life, and I felt the need of nothing or no one else. Let me say; I was fully occupied, and all my needs were being met. I was, as we say, "set for life."

Have you ever heard the saying, "Boy, I never saw that one coming?" Well, I was rather steeped in my spiritual comfort, experiencing financial miracles, enjoying Jesus and occasionally taking mission trips to other countries. What more did I need? Who else did I need? I had Jesus, and He was proving to be lavishly sufficient! Without warning, God was about to shake my world, redirect my life, enlarge my view and revise things to a measure that I never had before even imagined.

I will happily tell that story in the following chapter!

Chapter 8

Apprehended by a Huge Surprise

But as it is written: Eye has not seen, nor ear heard, nor have entered into the heart of man the things which God has prepared for those who love Him.

1 Corinthians 2:9

Before I tell you the promised story, permit me to give you some background information as I seek to weave a story of many single strands of Providence, seemingly totally unrelated, coming together in a surprising and astounding way, reminding us all once again that God knows everything about everything.

During the three months that I was privileged to stay at the home of Leif and Jennifer Hetland, I worked at the new office and began looking for a house. In my mind I wanted a place that had one or two extra bedrooms where I could entertain my children and grandchildren should they decide to come and visit me, as well as friends from out of town, to attend conferences at my new church and other churches in the area. While looking, I was praying that the Lord would sell my house in Columbus, Georgia to allow me to have a down payment for the new location; however, prior to the sale of the house, God led me to a brand new home under construction that was at the stage for me to decide whether I wanted hard wood flooring or carpet, selecting counter-tops and having fun fixing it up just like I wanted. I felt it was an ideal location for me on the outskirts of a small town near Florence, and I felt led to buy it. I must tell you; I was scared! This was such a huge responsibility I had embarked on and prayed that I would be able to fulfill my obligation to pay the lender.

The verse from the Bible came to my mind, and that frightened me even more.

> *Just as the rich rule the poor,*
> *so the borrower is servant to the lender.*
> Proverbs 22:7 NLT

I had never done this before. My late husband had taken care of all the documents necessary for the purchase of the house where I lived in Columbus. Then God directed my thoughts to a different verse in the Bible.

> *And my God shall supply all your need according*
> *to His riches in glory by Christ Jesus.*
> Philippians 4:19

When I signed the contract for the purchase in June of 2004, I felt such a peace coming over me followed by the absence of all fear and anxiety. I opted for a payoff within fifteen years instead of the usual thirty years after a reasonably sizeable down payment. I had just mentioned that I needed to sell the house in Columbus to enable me to have a down payment. No one came offering me a check or cash, and I cannot explain to you how it happened outside of God's care for me. However, besides the down payment I was not only able to make monthly mortgage payments but also doubled them and would have the house paid for within 7-1/2 years.

After the initial fear of assuming such a huge responsibility, all of a sudden I experienced a tremendous joy, because Jennifer and I really had some good times working on projects for the house together and selecting new furnishings. To God and His children, "new is good." What does the Bible say?

New wine calls for new wineskins.

Mark 2:22 NLT

I especially liked my time at breakfast where I was able to look out the window across the street at an open field where cows were grazing. Call me crazy, but they reminded me of the following Psalm of David:

The Lord is my shepherd;
I have all that I need.
He lets me rest in green meadows;
He leads me beside peaceful streams.
He renews my strength.
He guides me along right paths,
bringing honor to his name.
Even when I walk
through the darkest valley,
I will not be afraid,
for you are close beside me.
Your rod and your staff
protect and comfort me.
You prepare a feast for me
in the presence of my enemies.
You honor me by anointing my head with oil.
My cup overflows with blessings.
Surely your goodness and unfailing love will pursue me
all the days of my life,
and I will live in the house of the Lord forever.

Psalm 23 NLT

Each morning I looked forward to having breakfast with my Lord, my Shepherd. I was so in love with Him and still am. There is something about Him that will not allow me to let go! It seems as if He has laminated me to Himself. I like that word because it speaks of closeness and intimacy! That's how I felt toward Jesus.

As I mentioned earlier, I bought this house to be able to host family and friends from out of town that wanted to come to the various conferences. One of those was the *WordSpiritPower* conference with Dr. R.T. Kendall, Jack Taylor, and Charles Carrin that I had attended in 2003 where I had the privilege to get to know the team a little better and also see their spouses again that I had briefly met in Columbus. On this occasion, Jack's wife, Jerry, invited me to take a seat next to her during lunch and across from a lady who had been a pastor's wife and well acquainted with her and Jack. Jerry told us that we had something in common. During our conversation, the only thing I could determine that we had in common was that we were both widows. And that was it. Time went on, and I enjoyed working for Leif and being part of their family. I met some wonderful people in my new home church and was able to develop some great friendships.

As the year passed by so quickly, Christ Chapel Church hosted another *WordSpiritPower* conference in October 2004 with the previously mentioned three gentlemen, R.T. Kendall, Jack Taylor, and Charles Carrin. In the meanwhile, between the two conferences, Jerry, Jack's wife had died after only twenty-one months of marriage. I had previously heard of his misfortune and started to send a card of sympathy but decided against it lest he thinks that I was interested in a relationship with him. I had sympathy for him in his loss, but no feelings beyond that. Little did I know what an impact this particular conference would have on the rest of my life. As I have already said, "I never saw that one coming."

Surprised by Love

They say life is full of surprises. But every now and then there is a surprise of such magnitude that it proves to be ... well, as this discussion began, "It is the surprise of surprises!"

So here I was, a sixty-year-old widow with a single eye for Jesus and quite satisfied with His companionship and resourcefulness. The thought or mention of romance was as distant from my mind as Timbuktu. I had not a fig of interest in such, and if I had, I would have responded with, "Not a chance, not now or ever!" I would have pleasantly signed an affidavit that I would never, never engage in even thinking about romance in general or marriage in particular. The whole idea was far from my mind. I had served my time and had no intentions of repeating the past. I saw myself as a "widow," not a "single." "Widow" was good which meant, "been there, done that but never again!" Widow, yes! Wife? No, no and a thousand times no!

Have you noticed that God seems ever and anon to have a penchant for surprises? I sometimes feel that as He listens to people talk He is caught by such phrases as, "I will never ..." or "I wouldn't do this again come hell or high water ..." or "you won't ever find me doing that!" God seems to be drawn to words like "ever" and "never!"

I had not investigated the meaning of apprehension. I have found out that the English language is full of strange exceptions, paradoxes, and double meanings. The word "apprehension" means both "to catch" and "to understand," "to feel uneasy." Well, that was what was about to happen to me. The word "apprehended" covered the waterfront: "uneasy," "caught," and a strange mix of other feelings.

Enter Jack Taylor, spiritual father to Leif Hetland for whom I worked and for whose organization I gave direction. I knew Jack Taylor as a preacher and an author and highly esteemed as "Papa" of my boss, Leif. Our paths had crossed several times in the past!

I had first met Jack a few years earlier when he and his two colleagues held a *WordSpiritPower* conference in Columbus, Georgia, the city where I had lived all my life as a United States citizen. It was, in fact, the very first conference of its kind. Leif and Global Mission Awareness was one of the co-sponsors of the conference in Columbus.

Jack had recently lost his first wife to cancer and was grieving. I took note of the terrible loss in his life, had prayed for him but, in all honesty, that's as far as my thoughts went at that time about Jack Taylor. I simply knew him as a man of God who preached in conferences. I prayed for him with much concern, but the only relationship I had with him was through Leif, my spiritual mentor and boss and Jack's spiritual son.

Pardon another parenthesis

Now stay with me, because this is vital. Remember the words at the beginning of this chapter about the single strands of Providence? Well, the following is one of those many strands. A few months after Jack's first wife, Barbara, had passed, Leif on a spiritual "hunch" called Jack's secretary, Brenda Godson, to inquire of Jack's status and if fitting, offer a suggestion. The suggestion would have been that it might be God's will for Friede and Jack to be together. Brenda replied to Leif's suggestion that it might be too late since Jack was recently engaged. That was it … or was it? It is important that you know that neither Jack nor I were privy to this conversation. So put this in your hopper and hold on for a lesson in reality!

Now, it is the fall of 2004, and I was again attending a *WordSpiritPower* conference at a local church. I was standing at the end of the pew during the wonderful praises on the first night of the conference. It was at this point that the first of several occurrences came about that would radically change the direction of my life and every feature of my identity. Let me seek to tell it as it happened that unforgettable evening.

The service was in progress, and the congregation was standing, my hands were lifted toward heaven, when, at the corner of my vision, I caught sight of movement at the front of the church. I saw that Jack Taylor had walked out into the aisle and was walking toward the back of the Church. Now that I think about the event, what surprised me, yes even shocked me, was what I heard in my mind the moment I took note of his stepping into the isle. What I heard was as clear as the words on this page, "If he asks you to marry him, you will say, 'Yes'!" In my state of surprise and yes, even shock, I can guarantee you one thing: This thought and these words did not come from Friede McDonald. By now, he was no longer coming toward me; he was standing directly in front of me with his hands in a childlike pose, his voice exuding innocence, and his face reflecting kindness, his question was both soft and simple. "Would it be alright if we were to get together sometime next week?" As casually as he asked the question was the answer that escaped my lips with a partial smile, hiding inner surprise, I said: "Yes!" And that was it, or was it? Jack likes to describe my response as one of "noticeable glee." I think I would describe it more like a "what just happened?" I was in shock! Like a laser out of the blue. The results of this encounter were multiple questions for which there were no known answers.

What had just happened?

What was happening to me?

What did this man have in mind?

What did God have in mind?

These and other questions would be answered in a brief while!

To add to the already strange and mysterious circumstances was this significant fact: After my answer, Jack turned around to return to the front, the same voice that had spoken to me as Jack walked out into the isle toward me now sounded again, "He is the one, I am answering your prayer." My immediate response was, "But Lord, I did not pray for a husband!" to which He replied, "Remember Mozambique!" I stood in stunned silence thinking, "What about Mozambique?" More silence ... Then I remembered a scene two years prior at the Atlanta, Georgia Airport where Leif Hetland introduced me to two pastors who were accompanying us on the mission trip to Mozambique. I distinctly remember one of the pastors making a remark, "Before we get on this plane, let's make sure that everybody takes care of their own luggage." We then proceeded to our gate and began to prepare for the eighteen-hour flight to Johannesburg, South Africa. After a few hours in flight, the remark of that pastor came back to me. I was offended because I thought that the only reason he had said that was a reference toward me. He surely would not have said it if all the folks on the journey had been men. I could not ditch the offense; instead, it seemed to increase, so I began to talk to God about it. I said, "Lord, You are a wonderful husband, and there is no one out there like you, but if I would have had an earthly husband with me, that pastor would not have had cause to say those words. Therefore, if there is anyone out there like you, with skin on, that will love me like You do, that will have a passion for You as I do, who will not distract me from my passion for You or allow me to distract him from his passion for You, that will love to go on mission trips and agree to worship with me and pursue You individually at the same time, THEN YOU MAY BRING HIM MY WAY, BUT IF THERE IS NO ONE OUT THERE LIKE THIS, ALL I WANT IS YOU." Period! End of request! I never gave this prayer another thought until I heard the words, "He's the one, I am answering your prayer!" I responded, "But I really didn't mean that; I only said this because I was offended! I was not intentionally asking for a husband!"

Back to the Story

Rejoin me in the story at hand: I was by now a member of another church in the city and my Sunday was spent with my home church. I was so busy that I did not have much time to think about what happened the night before. But when I did think about it, my mind was flooded with questions and stunned with a bit of confusion, especially about what I heard as Jack walked toward me that night and further confused about what I heard when he returned to the front of the Church.

We, Leif, his wife Jennifer and I, attended the Monday morning session of the conference where all three preachers were sharing. As I looked at Jack, I had a faint feeling that something strange was happening, something beyond my comprehension, something that God knew that He wasn't telling me. Was I being "set up" and only God knew what was occurring?

After the service that Monday morning, Jack came back to where we had sat and this time approached Leif and asked, "Would it be all right if I took your secretary to lunch today?" The look on Leif's face was one of obvious shock, if possible more than mine. He glanced at me, then he glanced back at Jack, his face turning as white as the paper beneath these words. He had sudden recall of his conversation with Jack's secretary after the loss of his first wife. He then muttered softly and nodded in the affirmative. He had been right in what he heard, but wrong in his timing. He realized immediately that this meant that he was losing me as his office administrator. Jack loves to say that he, Jack, wrecked Leif's organization in one fell swoop. He was pleased that he had been right about us, but shocked about his perceived loss. He was victimized by his own prophecy!

Jack had received my affirmative answer on Saturday night. So on Monday, after Leif's consent, we went to a nearby restaurant and had thirty minutes together with a bit of food and conversation, all the time allowed as I had an appointment with my doctor. I don't remember the subject or content of the conversation, but I do remember that he reached both hands across the table and laid them over mine and remarked how beautiful my hands were. The plot thickens, as Jack asked me to be his guest at dinner after the service that evening with the speakers and Church staff. I was extremely uncomfortable as I sat among a group with whom I did not feel were my peers. The next day, Tuesday, it was lunch again with Jack. The questions still haunted me, "What is happening to me? Why is this man pursuing me? Could it be that he loves me? Can it be that I can love again?" Some excitement sprang up within me. My emotions were soaring and stirring. Could this be God or am I just touched by the interest of this unusual man? I was both pleased and unsurprised when he asked for another date for that evening. Something was awakening in me that had lain dormant for more than eleven years. The hope to love anyone but Jesus was not considered viable to my mind until the third date with Jack on Tuesday, October 19, 2004. Romantic love was not even on the table until this series of events that began on Saturday evening when the Holy Spirit spoke to me, "If he asks you to marry him, you will say, 'Yes!'" Jack's loving approach, deepening interest, the voice of Holy Spirit in my heart, with all my feelings in agreement, I knew that God had reset my table. I knew that this man was in love with me, and I was in love with him. Our fourth "date" was after the service Tuesday evening during which he posed the question, and I answered, "Yes!" Gleefully! (Jack's word! I agree!)

In this writing, Jack asked me to describe how I felt when I awakened on that Wednesday morning. Words fail me here. Excited? Yes! Peace? Total! Certain? Absolutely! Fulfilled? Incredibly! It is rather important that I say to you after eleven years, five months and sixteen days, at this writing, all these good words and a thousand others apply to my marriage to Jack Taylor! We were married seventy days after the proposal!

Disclaimer: Now to all the young people who may be reading this book and these words:

"Do not, and I repeat, do not try this at home!"
Our excuse? We were 131 years old and time was fleeting!
Differing circumstances determine differing choices!
Our story and we will stick to it!

The immediate Sunday following our decision to marry, I went to my church to worship and thanked God for all He had done during the past week. Our usual worship leader, Lenny LeBlanc was absent, and the worship team led the worship. During that time a young man named Scott sang a solo entitled "YOU RAISE ME UP," a song I had never heard before but made famous by Josh Groban. When I heard that song, I became overwhelmed with the realization of how much God loved me. I started to weep because I realized that it was God who now had raised me up to a new life, a new level, a life to be shared with a godly man, a man who had touched many lives in such a positive way.

Here are the lyrics of that song by which I was totally undone:

"When I am down, and, oh, my soul, so weary;
When troubles come, and my heart burdened be;
Then, I am still and wait here in the silence,
Until you come and sit awhile with me.

You raise me up, so I can stand on mountains;
You raise me up to walk on stormy seas;
I am strong when I am on your shoulders;
You raise me up to more than I can be.

There is no life - no life without its hunger;
Each restless heart beats so imperfectly;

But then you come, and I am filled with wonder,
Sometimes, I think I glimpse eternity.

You raise me up, so I can stand on mountains;
You raise me up to walk on stormy seas;
I am strong when I am on your shoulders;
You raise me up to more than I can be."

Immediate Collateral Effects

The first issues to appear, when such events as described in this chapter began to materialize, immediate family relationships come into view. This is both significant and inevitable. When two people, representing a number of family groups, join together in marriage, all sorts of potential concerns surface. The wisdom of God carefully applied and meticulously demonstrated forms the only answer to this complex picture. In my case, there were two children, Sheila, my daughter and Steve, my son. Adding to these primarily affected are their spouses and their children, resulting in rapidly increasing numbers. In my situation, those under this consideration amounted to a total of eleven significant human beings whose well-being, emotions and opinions must be respectably evaluated. In Jack's case, it was virtually the same, actually ten.

The reader will remember that my only daughter and I were estranged, her feeling being that I was drifting toward cultish behavior and that she was losing me. She strongly protested my traveling to foreign countries because of inherent dangers especially in cultures where women were perceived differently than in America. This painful estrangement was one reason for my being free to consider moving to help Global Missions Awareness and the Hetland's in their world-reaching ministry. Sadly, all communication between us had ceased. Despite this,

I felt that I must inform Sheila, my only daughter, about our sudden marriage plans. I knew that it was unlikely that she would pick up the phone, but I called her anyway. No answer. It was likely that she was home and simply choosing not to answer. So I voiced a simple message, "Sheila, this is your Mom, and I just wanted you to know that I'm getting married." The receiver was immediately lifted, and a voice on the other end said, "You whaaaaat?" I repeated my announcement that resulted in multiple questions.

Sheila: "Who is this you are marrying?"
Friede: "You wouldn't know him; his name is Jack Taylor."
Sheila: "How long have you known him?"
Friede: "Three or four years."
Sheila: "You never said anything about him. How long have you dated him?"
Friede: "Two days."
Sheila: "Are you crazy? Don't do anything!"
Friede: "He is a widower, in fact, he was married twice, and both wives died."
Sheila: "What did they die of?"
Friede: "They both died of cancer."
Sheila: "Don't you do anything, I want to check him out."

When I told Jack of this conversation, he offered to call her, and I thought this not to be a good idea. I was afraid that he would not be met with a kind reception. He called, and the conversation was cordial and resulted in plans for the family to meet Jack who would soon become their stepfather and step-grandfather. Sheila and her family were kind but cautious. It was decided that the soon-to-be Thanksgiving holidays were ideal for each of us to be with our respective families. No problem! Jack and I agreed and made plans accordingly to be with our separate families, he with his and I with mine. It proved to be a solid protocol. When we did get together, it was love at first sight on the part of all!

All possible ill will, and doubt, real and potential, seemed to melt like hot butter before a blazing sun, and my children and grandchildren readily accepted Jack, and he received them all as his very own family. It was nothing short of miraculous!

When I tried to call my son, Steve, to announce my marriage plans, he was not available. My daughter-in-law, Jennifer, answered the phone. Of course, I told her of the nature of my call. She immediately responded with an observation of caution with measured concern regarding the rapid decision, a caution I both appreciated and understood. My understanding of her concern was based on her love for me. When my son and I got together to discuss my marriage plans, his preference was that we wait until his upcoming deployment had ended so he could attend the wedding. We had proceeded with plans that we could not change. Though Steve and Jennifer were not able to attend the wedding, we felt that we had their approval.

It is both satisfying and safe for Jack and me to say that we are profoundly blessed that our families desire and enjoy our presence and want us to be happy together. We have made the decision, with firm agreement, to give each other the choice as to where we will spend the holidays, especially Thanksgiving and Christmas. This decision sometimes results in each of us being apart in order to spend that day with our own immediate family. After all, Jack and I joyously spend most of our time with one another due to the nature of our ministry. We never want our respective families to feel that they have less access to us because of one another.

A Second Collateral Effect

Though I had just purchased a new home in Alabama and

would have been glad for Jack to come there to live with me, it seemed obvious to both of us that the viable choice was in favor of my moving to Florida. Though I was under the impression that I would live the remainder of my life in Alabama, God had other plans for me! This necessitated the sale of my new home, purchased just five months earlier. After our wedding, we completed the move, and I moved into our lovely condominium on the beach of the Atlantic Ocean. Our home has an idyllic title: "Shalom Above the Sea!"

I am reminded of the command and promise in Matthew 6:33 (NLT):

Seek the Kingdom of God above all else, and live righteously, and he will give you everything you need.

Looking back, I saw that God had a purpose and a hand in all of this. He had a destiny for me and prepared the way for me to step into it.

Today I thank God that He has led me down a winding and sometimes rough road. It is this that has given me experiences with God's greatness and loving-kindness. My sorrows have enriched me with a wealth of knowledge that could not have been gained by any other means. My trials have been in the cleft of the rock in which God has set me, as he did his servant, Moses, that I might behold His glory as He passed by. A rock can be a truly hard place! I Praise God that I was not left to the darkness and ignorance, but that in the great fight of affliction, I have been enabled by the outshining of His glory in His wonderful dealings with me.

For I know the thoughts that I think toward you, says the Lord, thoughts of peace and not of evil, to give you a future and a hope.
Jeremiah 29:11

Ever since I made the decision to listen to and obey Jesus, He is allowing me to play in His Kingdom and watch Him do the work.

For the kingdom of God is not in word but in power.
1 Corinthians 4:20

In 2003 as I was visiting my mother in Germany we went to a Catholic Church together. Mama loved her church and attended every time she was able. On this day at the end of communion, the priest, as was the custom, returned the elements to the tabernacle and turned the key to lock the door. At the very moment that the key was turned, I experienced a sharp pain in my heart, and I heard the Lord say to me: "Now I am being locked up again until the next time when I am needed. I am not free to be myself." You see, the elements are a symbol of the presence of God. I began to weep right there in the pew sitting next to my mama. She wanted to know what was wrong with me and when I tried to explain it to her outside after the service, I could not make her understand. I was deeply grieved because there was a time when I wanted God only on my terms when I needed Him. At other times I simply locked Him out of my life. I then recognized that I had accepted His presence on my terms and I, as Frank Sinatra sang, "I did it my way."

Mama's Greatest Moment: Another Collateral Effect

In 2006 I flew to Germany to visit my then 91-year-old mother in the Catholic nursing home. As I entered the dayroom, all occupants where seated around a table with flowers in the middle of it and a crucifix in the center. One of the ladies told me that she wished I had come sooner as the Priest had been there and given them Holy Communion (or the Lord's Supper), but that he had not given it to the lady sitting across from her. I knew in my heart why, but I asked her why. She said because she was not a Catholic. That's when the Holy Spirit prompted me to speak up and tell them that Jesus died for all and that during His Last Supper commanded all His followers to "do this in remembrance of me," while referring to the bread as "my body" and the wine as "my blood." Then one of the ladies asked me: "Why has no one ever told us that?" Another lady said: "You need to preach that!" I would have said more, but it was time for the patients to receive their medications.

Later that afternoon, I took my mother outside in her wheelchair as the weather was beautiful and the sun was shining warmly. During this time, I heard my mother say that she was thinking about what I had said. When I asked her to be more specific, she simply stated that she needed and wanted Jesus. I wasted no time in putting the brakes on the wheelchair, getting down on my knees in front of her, holding her hand and leading her in a salvation prayer. She interrupted my prayer and proceeded with one of her own. I knew without a doubt, from the manner in which she prayed, that the transaction was done. There on the sidewalk in Stukenbrock, Germany on that sunny fall day my mama settled the issue of her certainty of heaven. Up until then, whenever I was leaving Germany to return home, I always said, "Mama, if we don't see each other again on this earth, I will see you in heaven," to which she invariably replied: "I hope so!" This has always caused me pain in my heart because there seemed the sad absence of certainty in her answer. I would tell her again and again, "Mama, the Bible says ..."

These things I have written to you who believe in the name of the Son of God, that you may know that you have eternal life, and that you may continue to believe in the name of the Son of God.

1 John 5:13

When the time came for my departure to America, I again said, "Mama, if I don't see you again on this earth, I will see you in heaven!" Her confident reply was a simple "Yes!" This was God's timing for mama's greatest moment on this earth and one of my greatest!

That very same evening my brother told me that he did not think it was worth my time and expense to come to Germany just to spend time with my mom in the nursing home. Someday I will be able to tell him why it was indeed worth all the time and money I could ever spend, a message he would not have understood had I told him that day. I would have gladly given ten times that amount just to hear my sweet mama share her heart with me and say yes to my proposal that I would see her in heaven. Three years later, after visiting her twice a year, I would hear her "yes!" for the last time. Some day, may be soon, I will see mama again and forever. Until then I will live overjoyed in the privilege of being a part of her certain salvation and having witnessed God bringing her into His Kingdom.

One of these days, I am excited to be part of my brother's coming to Christ as well. I have learned that my dependence on God changed my whole perspective. I see miracles happening all around, while others see only natural occurrences and "coincidences."

God sent His Son not only to save us to go to heaven but to bring heaven to earth and to do what Jesus did while He was on this earth,

The Spirit of the Lord is upon me because he has anointed me to proclaim good news to the poor. He has sent me to proclaim liberty to the captives and recovering of sight to the blind, to set at liberty those who are oppressed.
Luke 4:18 ESV

Heal the sick, raise the dead, cleanse the lepers,
cast out demons. Freely you received, freely give.

Matthew 10:8 BSB

Still More ...

I have been so blessed to be involved in salvations, healings and deliverances in Germany, Austria, Canada, Mozambique, Tanzania, Ivory Coast, Brazil, Cuba and Philippines and all over North America.

Yes, our God is the same yesterday, today and forever and the most exciting part is that He wants us to partner with Him. He has promised to give us the desires of our hearts! That means he places His desires within us so that our hearts are already beating with His!

Finding Lost Things

God is always interested in finding lost things. Jesus flatly stated His purpose when He said:

For the Son of Man has come to seek
and to save that which was lost.

Luke 19:10

In the confession of Jesus, we are acquainted with the fact that the reason for His coming centered upon something that had been lost. Jesus was revealing in this key passage the whole meaning of the Incarnation. The story of the Incarnation was and is a story of the ages. Nothing in the history of the human race compares with the magnitude of this incomprehensible mystery. No religion that ever existed or now exists or ever will exist can claim such an event and its accompanying effects on all the ages of time. It is not possible for the human mind to create such a narrative as God becoming man in order to abide by His Own plan with integrity. The existence of the Trinity of God, the Father, God, the Son and God, the Holy Spirit qualified this God alone as the One who could not only create the heavens and the earth, but also establish and sustain a system of laws to fulfill His plan and pursuit of His eternal purpose. Stop long enough to ask from whence did this God come? Who or what created Him, the creator of all that is? There is no answer available in man. God has ever been and will always be God, unopposed and uncreated. The one answer only creates more questions:

In the beginning God ...

Genesis 1:1a

We need not seek what was before that, because the answer is always, "God!" We should not ask because we need not ask. The benefits of this God are bound up in the narrative of the redemption. There was a wonderful beginning with matter, light, life, energy, time, plants, oceans, sea creatures, flying birds, crawling animals, stars, sun and moon. And God's response to His own creation was, "It is good!" He then created man and took from his side a rib from which He made the woman. He put them together and said, "This is very good!" But a thief was among them and in their disobedience stole something precious from them, the presence of God in the Garden. The whole story of the Bible is occasioned by God's restoring what was lost.

A Life of Surprises - Touching the Miraculous

Early in our marriage, I lost some rather costly diamond jewelry that Jack had given me. It disappeared on a ministry trip to Houston, Texas. I searched high and low, in my carry-on, in the liner of my carry-on, and even convinced myself that I might not even have brought it on the trip. I truly hoped that the hotel staff had not taken it. So, when we got home, I looked for it high and low and everywhere very carefully and thoroughly, without ever telling Jack about the loss. After the loss, I finally asked him if he had seen the jewelry, and he had not. I was so sad. It wasn't just the money it had cost, but the sentimental value of the expression of my husband's love. I actually grieved but tried to be careful not to allow slight grief to become worry.

Then a couple of weeks later we were ministering in Rochester, New York and I had already forgotten about the jewelry. Prior to the last service to be held Sunday evening, I decided to pack my suitcase with all the clothing except what I planned to wear to church that evening and on the flight home. Since I was in the habit of lining my suitcase with plastic prior to putting my clothes in it to keep them dry in the event of inclement weather, I just pulled the plastic over the clothes with the suitcase left open. When we returned to our hotel room after the Sunday night service, I decided to pack the clothes I had just worn. As I glanced at my suitcase, I noticed, to my amazement, that the jewelry box that had disappeared in Houston was resting on top of the plastic with which I covered my clothes. I was shocked and ecstatic! I even asked Jack if he had placed it there. He answered in the negative and asked me whether the jewelry was inside the box. I opened it, and there it was! My joy at the recovery of this jewelry was commensurate with the value I had assigned to it. My grief at the loss, at the same time, was the gauge of the measure of the value of the items lost. To me, this whole experience was of twofold significance. First, it simply made clear to me how absolute and thorough God's interest and involvement are with His children! Nothing is too small or insignificant to escape God's loving awareness. On the other hand, nothing is too large to challenge His ability to reverse the loss. Second, it served as a striking revelation of the value of my eternal relationship with my heavenly Father. The value of mere gold and silver pales in comparison to the gifts from God of forgiveness and eternal life.

I have been on the journey with God and His Kingdom long enough to understand that God will never put me through more than He and I can handle together. He will intentionally allow me to go through things I cannot handle, to teach me things that I could not otherwise learn. Besides this, it seems that God allows us to get into situations just to hear us cry "Help!" Feature a father teaching his child by demanding this child to do something the father knows he or she cannot do. The child engages in obedience and at last admits, "Father, I cannot do this by myself, will You help me?" The father has just demonstrated a vital principle of how God relates Himself to us. He knowingly puts on our agenda issues we cannot handle alone so that we can learn . . .

And God is able to make all grace abound toward you, that
you, always having all sufficiency in all things,
may have an abundance for every good work.
2 Corinthians 9:8

This book you are reading presents a clear example of what I have just written. My first language was German. I have had no formal training in English grammar or parts of speech. Jack has a minor in college English and often asks me for advice in both spelling and grammar. That is a miracle! I was forced by circumstances to learn English, circumstances allowed by a loving God. The ways of God include allowing us to experience situations of need in order to deliver to us His riches in Jesus! What a wonderful God!

I am grateful for a relationship with God that is filled with surprises. He tells us only part of the story and reveals the rest along the way through experiences of need, pressure, and surprises.

Doxology

Father, I thank you for your faithfulness. I thank you for your amazing love that knows no boundaries. You were willing to go to extremes to bring us life everlasting, and You sometimes go to extremes with us because You love us and want us so close to Your heart that we get to know its beat and in that beat, we find comfort, peace, and joy. We cannot find that by our might or by our power, but only by Your Spirit. So Father, release your Holy Spirit on us now and draw us ever closer so that we can truly say amid all the circumstances in this life that, "FOR ME TO LIVE IS CHRIST, TO DIE IS GAIN."

In Jesus' Name. Amen

Chapter 9

A Chapter I Never Intended to Write

*To the Jews who had believed him, Jesus said, "If you hold to
my teaching, you are really my disciples. Then you will know
the truth, And the truth will set you free."*
John 8:31-32 NIV

As mentioned earlier in this book, I was born in the fading
days of Nazi Germany, just over a year before Hitler took his
own life that effectively marked the end of Hitler's mad dream
of world domination. I never knew enough about Hitler in my
early years to hate him or fear him. But I did begin to learn of
the scope and magnitude of the influence of one of the most
evil tyrants the world has ever known. I came to know that,
because of this man's evil schemes matched with a brilliance
and determination beyond imagination, those who obeyed him
as their leader terminated millions of lives deliberately. I was
soon to know that millions more died across the world amid
the ravages of wars initiated by Adolf Hitler. It is interesting to
know that in the days of the first half of the twentieth century
Hitler's imposing presence and evil plans formed an undeniable
specter of fear and terror over the entire world.

In spite of all this, I remain connected, not only by the
memories of my life but by the presence of loved ones who have
remained in Germany's continuous reconstruction and recovery
from those most tragic years. It remains the country of my
beginning. I am now an American and after more than half a
century I love my country. But through the years in traveling to

and from my home country, I still appreciate its beauty and its meaning in my life.

A New Thought Pattern

As noted in the title of this chapter, a new thought was presented that captured my imagination and I became very intrigued with questions about the country of my previous citizenship. Questions that arose were the following:

1. How did Germany rise to power among the nations of the world?
2. How was this greatness marred by the evil plans of one man?
3. What ideologies influenced Hitler that produced one of the most destructive schemes in the history of man?
4. Who were those who might have influenced Adolf Hitler to become driven by the thought that there was a final solution in the progress of civilization that resulted in the annihilation of more than six million human beings he could find of Jewish descent?
5. What lessons can we learn from Hitler's Germany that would ensure us against ever repeating its tragic holocaust?

It is here that I dare to enter thoughts that have come to me in the last few hours. I am a loyal citizen of what I consider to be the greatest nation on the face of the earth, the United States of America, while I still hold a love for the country of my youth, a country I have enjoyed returning to more than forty times over the last five decades.

My mind is now racing as I consider those searching questions, having come to feel that a chapter I never intended to write must be written. I will not attempt in this writing to answer the questions above in detail. Such an attempt would only foster other unanswerable questions. What I will do is insert into the narrative certain thoughts that I consider to be pertinent and relevant in the twenty-first century. If we are to be prepared to face the uncertain future, it is good to have light and understanding of issues from the past. Thus, in the remainder of this chapter, the words *perhaps* or *what if* will be employed; denoting thoughts entertained and questions begging appropriate answers. In the search engines I am using, names are appearing that I have never before connected. Obviously the name Adolf Hitler, sometimes simply called Hitler or "The Führer," is the most obvious and certainly the most tragic. A common adage is that no man is an island. Thought patterns and influences in early age, middle age and following are a part of a person's life. As I have thought to acquaint myself today with those who have influenced the culture of Germany, both for good and evil, I have run across two names that have especially intrigued me. These two men are a part of the history of Germany.

One of them was a very evil man who was dead set against God, Christianity, and the Church, who discounted the whole idea of the Christian religion as idiotic, untenable and damaging to civilization. His name was Friedrich Wilhelm Nietzsche. Nietzsche was a man of great brilliance and an articulate speaker regarding his ideologies. He felt it to be one of the great accomplishments of his life if he could destroy the whole idea, in one fell swoop, of God, Jesus, and Christianity. Most of his writings have survived a period of time approaching one hundred and fifty years and remain available to this day. As I have engaged in this study, it is apparent, in my mind, that whether or not we have been reading Nietzsche's work, our present civilization in the west and perhaps in all the world, is being influenced by his line of thought and worldview. Above every war, conflict and skirmish currently being waged, that which stands paramount between good and evil is the campaign being waged over the minds of mankind in the twenty-first century. At the root of all these conflicts are the issues of God's existence as the creator, sustainer, and ruler of the world. As a result of this, the inevitable questions that must be asked are:

1. Does God exist?
2. If there is such a God as Christianity claims, what are our options?

Our answer will inevitably affect every last life of the more than seven billion people on Planet Earth. If we agree with Nietzsche, our decision is made, and we can take his position that was attributed to him long after his death, "God is dead!" As we leave Nietzsche, I call you to remember that this man, at forty-four years of age, entered the slippery slope of mild insanity that worsened until his mind gave into total insanity and imprisoned his whole being until his death at fifty-five.

If I could give an epitaph to Nietzsche's life, it would be that of John Greenleaf Whittier:

"Of all sad words of tongue or pen, the saddest are these,
'It might have been.'"

Nietzsche died as he lived, hopeless and without purpose, exhibiting the absurdity of a life without God. No thinking person would, in the light of this misguided mind and his life's tragic closing chapter, choose to follow such a philosophy. However, at this present moment, there are untold thousands of people, who, by deliberate decision or thoughtless drift are guided by this destructive dismissal of God from human thought.

As we leave the regrettable story of this brilliant, but misguided life, we should remember that history has recorded the fact that Nietzsche's worldview was strategic in shaping the landscape of Hitler's Germany. Of that, we can be safely certain.

Now let us turn to another fabled life, that of Dietrich Bonhoeffer, another German and another seeker of truth whose life was taken at the end of a hangman's rope at Flossenbürg concentration camp under the command of Adolf Hitler. Bonhoeffer, at thirty-nine years of age, only days before the American liberation of the POW camp, became arguably the most famous martyr of the twentieth century. His famous lines offer evidence of the nature of his philosophy and the depth of his faith:

"A God who let us prove his existence would be an idol."

~~~~~~~~~~~~~~~~

"Do not try to make the Bible relevant. Its relevance is axiomatic.
Do not defend God's Word, but testify to it. Trust to the Word.
It is a ship loaded to the very limits of its capacity."

~~~~~~~~~~~~~~~~

"Silence in the face of evil is itself evil: God will not hold us guiltless. Not to speak is to speak. Not to act is to act."

~~~~~~~~~~~~~~~~

"Judging others makes us blind, whereas love is illuminating.
By judging others, we blind ourselves to our own evil and to the grace which others are just as entitled to as we are."

~~~~~~~~~~~~~~~~

"Jesus himself did not try to convert the two thieves on the cross;
he waited until one of them turned to him."

~~~~~~~~~~~~~~~~

"The ultimate test of a moral society is the kind of world that it leaves to its children."

~~~~~~~~~~~~~~~~

"We must be ready to allow ourselves to be interrupted by God."

~~~~~~~~~~~~~~~~

"In ordinary life, we hardly realize that we receive a great deal more than we give, and that it is only with gratitude that life becomes rich."

~~~~~~~~~~~~~~~

"I'm still discovering, right up to this moment, that it is only by living completely in this world that one learns to have faith. I mean living unreservedly in life's duties, problems, successes and failures, experiences and perplexities. In so doing, we throw ourselves completely into the arms of God."

~~~~~~~~~~~~~~~

"The will of God, to which the law gives expression, is that men should defeat their enemies by loving them."

These quotations were taken from the writings of Dietrich Bonhoeffer. This man died, as did Nietzsche, as he lived. The latter died in abject hopelessness and helpless insanity, descending further into darkness. The testimony of his life without God was complete.

To the contrary, Dietrich Bonhoeffer, imprisoned for his alleged role in the failed assassination plot on Adolf Hitler's life in 1944, was recorded as saying:

"How should one become arrogant over successes or
shaken by one's failures when one shares in God's
suffering in the life of this world?
You understand what I mean
even when I put it so briefly.
I am grateful that I have been allowed this insight,
and I know that it is only on the path that I have finally
taken that I was able to learn this.
So I am thinking gratefully and with peace of mind
about the past as well as present things.
May God lead us kindly through these times,
but above all, may God lead us to himself."

His final recorded words before his hanging were:

"This is the end for me – the beginning of life."

Contrary to Nietzsche, descending into darkness, Bonhoeffer ascended into light! My reason for referring to these two lives who influenced my beloved Germany, one for evil, the other for good, is to spotlight "the rest of the story," a resounding parable of ultimate good over evil. Nietzsche's body lies in a little-noticed grave in a churchyard near where his father once preached the gospel his son so decisively denounced. The few fans of Nietzsche who come to visit on occasion quietly visit it. It is rather certain that his "God is dead" assertion was a major influence toward not only the beginning of the Nazi devastation of much of Europe, but also the revival of the title as a theme of the short-lived movement late in the twentieth century.

The grave of Dietrich Bonhoeffer exists amid mystery. It is believed that he was either buried in a mass grave with others who were hanged with him or his body burned and his ashes scattered on the ground. Regardless of what is believed about his grave, what we do know is that his life and death formed a clear and lasting testimony to the power of the Gospel of Jesus Christ, which, at this moment, is resounding loudly across the world through his works, his biographies and current articles appearing in leading Christian periodicals. What was said of Abel of old is a fitting sketch of Dietrich Bonhoeffer,

He being dead, yet speaks.
Hebrews 11:4

Because of my stated intention to influence people with my story, I ask you to take a journey with me in your imagination. Before we do that, let us remember that in the early history of the world there were four human beings on this planet: Adam and Eve and their children, Cain and Abel. Sin had caused their parents to be dismissed from paradise, and the gate of the garden was shut to them and their offspring. Sin was not only an event in history; it was the beginning of a disease that would be a permanent pandemic in every culture as long as time existed. Everyone who has read the Bible knows the familiar story of Cain and his brother Abel. Sin and all its expressions had invaded the human race. Jealousy, a cardinal sin, caused a conflict between Cain and Abel. As with all sins, the ultimate expression of jealousy is death. It is not an incidental fact that the truth, flatly stated, is

The wages of sin is death.
Romans 3:23

Have you noticed the boldness of the incorrect grammar in that sentence? This is a flagrant and inexcusable violation of grammar. It should be "the wages of sin are death" instead of is death. If you have not examined this violation of grammar, you need to, right now! Wages are something someone pays for a response. When our response is sin or a violation of God's law, the result is death. Spiritual truth transcends grammar. Sins' wages ultimately amount to one thing: DEATH! Cain, in a fit of jealousy, killed his only brother and in doing so terminated twenty-five percent of the world's population and life on earth became a culture of death. With this startling realization, please join me on an imaginary trip through the universe.

Imagine yourself on a journey with me on a spacecraft through the vastness of the universe. Time and words would fail to describe what we would see on such a journey at the speed of thought with unlimited understanding.

No one on this journey would lack excitement as our Guide informs us that we are approaching our own birthplace, the only planet, so far amid the billions of others, on which life has been found. Located in a galaxy called the Milky Way, one of the smaller galaxies among the billions of other galaxies, we see the earth looming in our view. It is strangely small, blue in color and introduced simply as Earth. The Guide seems moved with great emotion, as a description of this strange planet is about to take place. We are also moved as we recognize our kinship to this strange blue planet. Time seems to slow and all but stop as the Guide says. "This is God's strategic project that was created to influence His whole cosmic enterprise, but something went awry, and the violation of God's law suddenly infected the entire planet with a dread disease: Death." Imagine the Guide, with seriousness of tone and deliberateness of speech, every word weighted with relevance, as we find ourselves seeing, as never before, the truth of a statement of which we all are aware,

You shall know the truth, and the truth shall make you free.
John 8:32

We hear in certain tones the truth about everything: creation, time, light, energy, matter, purpose and destiny and yes, sin, salvation, new heavens and new earth and everything else! The spacecraft lands, the door opens, the ramp is lowered and One Whose countenance shines with the brightness of a thousand suns is waiting for us and from His lips come the words "Welcome home." For the first time, what we have apprehended by faith alone, now we comprehend completely!

Why this astonishing imaginative journey? Because, this is the destiny of all who know God, the Creator, Jesus, our Savior, and the Holy Spirit, our Guide. And suddenly we will realize the absoluteness of our God, the reality of our faith and the meaning of eternity. And with these discoveries it dawns on us that nothing, absolutely nothing, and no one, was created by this great God, lacking purpose. The questions about nations, races, and divisions of mankind that were introduced in the earlier part of this chapter are all answered when we know then as we are known.

For now we see in a mirror, dimly, but then face to face.
1 Corinthians 13:12a

We will then know for sure that all the bloodshed of the thousands of years of human history, all the heartaches and heartbreaks of time have disappeared and we realize, as never before, that indeed, the answer to all our searches and what we have believed by faith, has become ultimate reality. What has made no sense during the years of our lives, now for the first time, makes perfect sense as we allow the mind of Christ to unfetter our thoughts.

Our trip has ended. We have observed the collateral blessings that are soon to be realized, and the planet, pervaded by truth and hope, becomes the culture of hope.

Now may the God of hope fill you will all joy
and peace in believing, that you may abound
in hope by the power of the Holy Spirit.
Romans 15:13

Chapter 10

From History to Destiny

*... Forgetting the past and looking forward to what lies
ahead, I press on to reach the end of the race
and receive the heavenly prize for which God,
through Christ Jesus, is calling us.*
Philippians 3:13b-14 NLT

Establishing and Keeping a Balance

Paul sets a classic example for all of us in evaluating the past, celebrating the present, and anticipating the future. Without being overly conscious of it, this work on my life has brought me to the awareness of the need of arriving at a place, establishing a perspective and maintaining a proper balance between the past and the future. To live in the past is pointless. To live in the future is impossible. To live in the present is our only viable choice. When Paul said, "Forgetting the past ..." he was acknowledging the inevitable, namely remembering the past. For me, it has been a wonderful journey with stopovers at pleasant places and friendly people and seeming tragedies with many tears. I have become aware of the truth of Malcom Muggeridge's claim in his late years that most of the beneficial things he had learned where the fruits of his sufferings and stress. His words deserve our attention:

"As an old man ... looking back on one's life,
it's one of the things that strikes you most forcibly—
that the only thing that's taught one anything is
suffering.

Not success, not happiness, not anything like that.
The only thing that really teaches one what life's all
about … is suffering and affliction."

"Every happening, great and small,
is a parable whereby God speaks to us,
and the art of life is to get the message."

The tears of sorrow, disappointment, and grief, properly understood, can turn into tears of joy, gratitude, and expectation, all depending on the ability as to when to remember and when to forget. We will find often and ever again that the worst scenes of our former years were just a few steps from the greatest victories. The scalding tears from the hurts we were enduring found us discovering that those same tears turned into the pleasant cleansing of our souls and into tears of delightful praise.

Let me illustrate: the bitter tears of rejection from a father unable or unwilling to love me became tears of overwhelming joy when I found God as the perfect Father.

The deep wounds inflicted by a husband, who, in the earlier years of our marriage, seemed to take his pain out on his wife and children, were soon to become reasons for delight as God took over his life.

The sudden shock of a son's suicide, once accepted and received, was upgraded with the certain expectation of seeing him again some glad day.

The pangs of loneliness and loss of a husband were but introductions to the joys of loving again and finding fresh destiny in ministry. Peter wrote:

After you have suffered for a little while, the God of all grace, who called you to His eternal glory in Christ, will Himself perfect, confirm, strengthen and establish you.

1 Peter 5:10 NAS

The operative words in Paul's promotion "reaching forward to what is ahead", an action that requires simply getting up and moving on, leaving one place to go to another. It is a dreadful thing to be locked in a parenthesis of painful mystery. The greater tragedy is to stay where we are. We do well to take note of the four leprous beggars referred to in 2 Kings, Chapter Seven, whose conversation is recorded for our benefit. Whether they individually spoke reflecting wise logic together or one at a time, we are given the greatest formula for turning tragedy into triumph. The four issues of that logic, when kept in mind, move us from where we are, closer to where we should be. The most important issue in this story is that when the exercise of simple logic and subsequent action were practiced, the large city was rescued, an episode that surely lifted four pitiful rejects to sudden fame as heroes.

During this writing, my husband, Jack, preached on this text that tells this intriguing and unforgettable story. He gave consent for its use here. I had heard him preach the sermon before but his whole emphasis, this time, was on the one thing that was accomplished—the breaking of a massive siege that had caused great loss of life and many shocking, devastating scenarios. There are times when events in the Bible leave us puzzled as to why they appear in the narrative. In the course of time and events, there are happenings and situations that put light on random people or simple truths. Eternity alone will reveal how seasons were changed in a seemingly coincidental act, statement, or unintended reaction.

A city is under siege; people are dying, many already dead. The stench of rotting corpses and the cries of weeping women fill the atmosphere. A busy metropolis has ground to a dull and dreary halt. A mammoth army surrounds the city, choosing to allow the city to die instead of invading and slaughtering the population. Something must happen!

At this sad juncture four sad, forsaken and dying lepers show up at the gates of the city. Their conversation is recorded for us to read several thousand years down the line. We might have expected the king and his cabinet or the priest and his wise men or the city fathers and their counselors together in their lofty throne rooms, in their studies or walking in paths of learning. But this was not to be. Instead we find four pitiful, gaunt and emaciated lepers, stumbling forward toward the city gates, more dead than alive, at the bottom of the food chain, mumbling among themselves. Had we been looking for heroes that day, we would have passed them by without a thought! Let's imagine the conversation:

The first point of logic was: **"We can't stay here!"**
The second point of logic was: **"We can't go back!"**

The correctness of these two conclusions erased certain options and isolated the next option: If we can't stay here and we can't go back, that leaves only the third option: **We have to go "on!"** Then another issue arises: where is "on?" When you think about it, it is rather easy to identify. It is the opposite of where we have been and where we are. It is, despite its uncertainty, bound to produce results. The only problem there is that there is a good chance that the results will be tragic, i.e., the enemy may kill us. A philosophical attitude will determine the report: well, they died trying. You know the story. The best possible scenario, their actions took them into a camp recently vacated by a gigantic army that had been aroused by what they thought was the sound of a marching army. Just as they were sitting down to engage in a sumptuous meal, the sounds, the sights, the glaring lights in the night caused terror and panic and resulted in flight, the whole army going AWOL! The lepers' next choice was a no-brainer; they sat down and ate until they could eat no more. This was followed by frenetic discoveries of compound riches. They filled their pockets with gold and silver. They loaded their arms with clothing and began to hide their loot. It was then that the fourth element came into view. **"This is not right, we do not well, this is a day of good news, and we remain silent."** Then they did something that won the day! They told their story, they reported their discovery, and they announced the good news. Confusion, starvation, and destruction have all come to an end. Look at their formula. Apply it to your life today. What happened to them and for them will happen to you!

There are some things we need to review to insert this thought process into our inner culture. I wish I might have had this protocol of options earlier on in my life. There were times when I had no sense of any viable options. Giving up hope when confusion comes is the most dangerous option that can be exercised. Giving up will keep us from getting up and going on with no hope. We cannot live long without hope.

In the event that the reader is among those who have either given up all hope or is considering such, review the following:

Our story is about a city and a territory on the verge of stark hopelessness and total destruction. Everyone left alive is hungry. A few are left who were even struggling for hope. Everyone else is waiting to die. The issue that is brought to us in this episode is that something has happened that changed a seemingly impossible situation from tragedy to victory. The siege is suddenly broken by four lepers, unnamed and unnoticed, who reasoned amid their desperation and found determination to pursue their conclusions. Their conclusions were:

> First, **"We cannot stay here!"**
> Second, **"We cannot go back!"**
> Third, **"We must get up and go on!"**

This is the place of great risk and while the rule of probability is that death is just ahead, anything is worth a try. You know the story. To review it, read 2 Kings Chapter 7. They were saved.

They were satisfied. They were set for life at its best, but for one thing, nobody in the city knew the good news. Enter the glad finish that chronicles the saving of a city.

Fourth, "We do not well, good things are happening, and we are not telling about them."

I have entered this chapter for the very purpose of telling you, the reader, that there is always hope! I have been in a litany of circumstances, flanked by thoughts of throwing in the towel, giving up and giving in to hopelessness. The list has included a father whose rejection was constant, every day for the first seventeen years of my life. His death by his own hand later, a husband turned alcoholic amid the terrors of war, overwhelming problems of adjusting to a new culture, the suicide of a son, a husband taken by cancer and many other issues that included a daughter diagnosed with cancer, a son assigned to the war-torn Middle East and the death of a precious mom. But for God, I would not have made it. And here I am telling you, "There is hope!"

May the God of hope fill you with all joy and peace as you trust in him so that you may overflow with hope by the power of the Holy Spirit.
Romans 15:13 NIV

A Final Review

From the beginning to now you have followed me on my journey to my destiny. Though there is a single destiny in the heart of God for all of us, there is a uniqueness about the destiny in His heart for each of us. We are not copies like identical twins or triplets, but we are originals with our own God-given

DNA and identity. While the roads, landscapes, weather and the surroundings, in general, are varied and unique, our supreme purpose and end are to discover and be fitted into God's eternal Kingdom pattern. This involves our passionate pursuit to find our place in God's overall plan and the means of sustaining our relationships with Him and His Kingdom family. While the means will inevitably vary and the events and conditions will differ, the ultimate purpose at the end of time will be realized at the Throne of God, from which He and we will reign forever over the vast and rapidly expanding cosmos. Then the glad realization will dawn on us that all along, every event, every incident, every tear of sadness and loss and every sound of laughter and joy have all been part of the cosmic scheme of our Creator, the God of heaven, to prepare us to reign with Him forever and ever! He who lives in us to reign in life on earth will ultimately welcome us to our place in Him on the throne to reign throughout the universe forever.

Welcome to your destiny and mine ...
On the throne with Him!

I pray that what I have shared with you over these pages may comfort you, challenge you and move you to a greater desire for an ever increasing passion and pursuit of your personal destiny in Him.

"Jesus Shall Reign Where'er the Sun"
by Isaac Watts (1674-1748)

"Jesus shall reign where'er the sun
Does his successive journeys run,
His kingdom stretch from shore to shore
Till moons shall wax and wane no more.

For Him shall endless prayer be made,
And endless praises crown His head;
His name, like sweet perfume, shall rise
With ev'ry morning sacrifice.

People and realms of ev'ry tongue
Dwell on His love with sweetest song;
And infant voices shall proclaim
Their early blessings on His name.

Blessings abound where'er He reigns;
The pris'ner leaps, unloosed his chains,
The weary find eternal rest,
And all the sons of want are blest.

Where He displays His healing power,
Death and the curse are known no more;
In Him the tribes of Adam boast
More blessings than their father lost.

Let every creature rise and bring
Peculiar honors to our King;
Angels descend with songs again,
And earth repeat the loud Amen."

Hymn #511
The Lutheran Hymnal
Text: Psalm 72
Author: Isaac Watts, 1719, cento
Composer: John Hatton, 1793
Tune: "Duke Street"

About the Author

Friede Taylor was born in Czechoslovakia the third child of a Catholic family during WWII. The deprivations and unsanitary conditions brought about by the war left her severely ill with typhoid fever and cholera, reducing her prospects for survival as a child. Because of overcrowded hospital facilities, she was left to die. Her father had been taken prisoner by the US Army, leaving Friede's family alone without support. A nurse had pity on them and took them into her home, giving Friede blood transfusions, using her (the nurse's) own blood to save Friede's life.

Her father was released at the end of the war, and the family moved to Germany where she suffered for years from rejection because her father had wanted her to be a boy. Her father, a tailor, lost everything in the war and died by his own hand without ever telling Friede that he loved her.

At 19, Friede married a US soldier stationed in Germany and moved with him to Columbus, Georgia where they raised a family of three children. In 1979, Friede converted from Catholicism to Southern Baptist where she accepted Jesus Christ as her Lord and Savior.

In 1983, after her oldest son, Gene, took his own life, Friede experienced what she calls an open-heaven experience with God's comfort and protection over her life—an experience which comforted her in future losses. Her husband died of cancer after 30 years of marriage, leaving Friede widowed for the next 11 years.

In 1999 she had a life-changing experience with the Holy Spirit, discovering God to be the Father who loved her and Husband who provided for her every need. Her pursuit of God brought her to a commitment and a passion for a deeper intimacy with God.

In 2004, she moved to Florence, Alabama by God's divine direction and became Director of Missions for Global Missions

Awareness. She has ministered in Mozambique, Tanzania, Philippines, and Cuba with Leif Hetland, GMA Founder, and President, and was scheduled to travel to Pakistan with GMA when Jesus and Jack Taylor derailed her plans.

She and Jack suddenly realized God's hand in bringing them together in October of 2004. They were married in less than three months with multiple confirmations from God that this was His will, and she moved to live with Jack in Melbourne, Florida, following their wedding.

Friede is Vice President of Dimensions Ministries and travels with Jack, ministering at every opportunity. Friede carries an intense burden and passion for the lost and broken people of the world. Her testimony is filled with power and pathos and all who hear her are moved by the faithfulness of God in her behalf.

Contact Friede at her website:

FriedeTaylor.com